LIVE LIKE A CHAMPION TODAY:

THE 40 PROMISES IN 40 DAYS CHALLENGE!

Dr. Jerry D. Ingalls

LIVE LIKE A CHAMPION TODAY:
THE 40 PROMISES IN 40 DAYS CHALLENGE!

Copyright © 2022 Dr. Jerry D. Ingalls

Published by Northside Books & Media, an imprint of AGF Publishing LLC.

All Scripture references are from The New American Standard Bible: 1995 Update (La Habra, CA: The Lockman Foundation, 1995), unless otherwise noted.

ISBN: 978-1-955709-07-1

DEDICATION

I dedicate this book to the many coaches I have been blessed by over the years. First, thank you to Coach Robert LaBreche of South Windsor High School, who represents to me the best of the many coaches and positive influences of my childhood years. Second, thank you to Coaches Jerry Quiller and Greg Gassner of West Point Track & Field, who were the tip of the spear of the many great people who invested in me at the Academy. Finally, thank you to the many positive influences upon me during my time in All-Army Sports, the US Army's World Class Athlete Program, and USA Track & Field. A special thank you to Dr. Nate Zinsser, my performance psychologist, who imparted confidence to me during my time at the Academy and as I trained for the Olympics. I am humbled and blessed to have been influenced by so many champions throughout my life. Each person has taught, encouraged, and inspired me to be my very best and to live like a champion today!

Soli Deo Gloria!

CONTENTS

Section 3 The Precious and Magnificent Promises of God!

ACKNOWLEDGMENTS

This book is for God's glory and the building up of His people through the teaching of the promises of God! It is for these two reasons that much of this material was first developed for my preaching ministry at First Baptist Church of New Castle, Indiana. The leadership agreed in the Spirit that we needed to focus the hearts and minds of our beloved congregation on the promises of God, and build them up with faith, hope, and love, for their daily living. I testify that preaching and teaching on the promises of God has been for such a time as this, as we have witnessed so many good people regain their mental focus and emotional well-being after being distracted and discouraged by the COVID-19 pandemic for so long. I encourage any pastor, church leader, or parachurch leader who has this book to use this material not only for the strengthening of your personal spiritual vitality, but also for the equipping of God's people in the various ways this book could be utilized for personal growth, small group discussions, and the corporate gatherings of local assemblies.

There are so many people at FBC who play an important role in my pastoral ministry. We are better together in Jesus! Thank you to the amazing officers, ministry leaders, staff members, volunteers, and members of our faithful congregation. Truly, FBC is richly blessed with good people who love the Lord and are very supportive of me, and my family, in our calling from the Lord to serve them in pastoral ministry. I am humbled by God's grace through each of you!

Specifically, for the writing of this book, I am thankful for Emily Hurst, a thoughtful leader in our congregation, and a gifted editor, who edits my weekly sermons and occasional books. I am better because of our partnership! I am thankful for Sean Slagle, a faithful brother, and my amazing publisher, who believes in me and my material. It is with deep gratitude for him, his persistent encouragement for me to publish, and his company, AGF Publishing LLC, that I am able to get this work into the hands of a larger readership. Thank you to Will, Christy, and Tytus Ragle for providing valuable input on the book's cover design and the final order of the book's sections. While I take responsibility for the content of this book, and any errors that are found within it, I recognize that without either Emily or Sean, and the support of the leadership and congregation of FBC, this book would not be in your hands today.

Finally, I want to thank my wife, Kimberly, and our three children, Beorn, Alana, and Willow, for loving me and being an amazing family. I love each of you, and I couldn't imagine doing life or ministry without you! I am blessed to have such a supportive and loving family, just as we are privileged to have First Baptist Church of New Castle, Indiana as our church family. Above all, I give Jesus Christ the preeminence in all things, and I acknowledge that if there is anything of value, or worthy of praise, in this book, it is only by God's grace – for His glory alone!

Praise God, from whom all blessings flow.
Praise Him, all creatures here below.
Praise Him above, ye heavenly host.
Praise Father, Son, and Holy Ghost.
Amen.

Dr. Jerry D. Ingalls

INTRODUCTION

The Bible emphasizes that a 40-day period has significance. The spies spent 40 days checking out the Promised Land. When the people didn't follow the report of Caleb and Joshua to trust God to fulfill His promises, they were disciplined with a 40-year period of wandering in the desert so that they could learn how to trust that God always provides for that which God promises. Jesus spent 40 days in the wilderness at the beginning of His Earthly ministry and 40 days at the end of His Earthly ministry, after His resurrection and before His ascension, teaching His followers about the Kingdom of God. Forty is a biblical number.[1]

While there is no magic to this number, 40 days is a significant amount of time to either change a habit or be well on the way to solidifying a new one. My hope for you as you embark upon the journey of learning how to live like a champion today is that you will take the "40 Promises in 40 Days Challenge!" and learn how to live a victorious life with God by learning to trust God and walk in His promises in your everyday life. In other words, my goal is for you to learn how to live like a champion today!

---

1 Here is a succinct biblical account of examples of the 40-day period: "During the flood it rains for 40 days and 40 nights (Gen. 7:4, 12, 17; 8:6). Moses is on the mountain for 40 days and nights (Exod. 24:18; 34:28; Deuteronomy 9). The spies spend 40 days in the land of Canaan (Num. 13:25; 14:34). The prophet Elijah takes 40 days and nights to reach the mountain of God in Sinai (1 Kgs. 19:8). Jesus fasts 40 days and nights in the wilderness (Matt. 4:2; Mark 1:13; Luke 4:2). Jesus spends 40 days with his disciples prior to his ascension (Acts 1:3). (2) Years. Both Isaac and Esau marry at the age of 40 (Gen. 25:20; 26:34). The Israelites eat manna in the wilderness for 40 years (Exod. 16:35), the time of the entire wandering in the wilderness (Num. 14:33–34; 32:13; Deut. 2:7; 8:2; 29:5; Josh. 5:6). The Israelites are subject to the Philistines for 40 years because of their sinfulness (Judg. 13:1). Many of the kings are said to have reigned for 40 years (David, 2 Sam. 5:4; Solomon, 1 Kgs. 11:42; Jehoash/Joash, 2 Kgs. 12:1; 2 Chr. 24:1; Saul, Acts 13:21)" (Michael Joseph Brown and Calvin L. Marion, "Measuring Time," in *The Eerdmans Companion to the Bible*, ed. Gordon D. Fee and Robert L. Hubbard Jr. [Grand Rapids, MI; Cambridge, U.K.: William B. Eerdmans Publishing Company, 2011], 69).

Are you up for the challenge?

I love a good challenge, and every athlete I've ever known has loved a good challenge. Athletes love challenges because we know that it is only through stretching ourselves that we can discipline our bodies, push our limits, channel our emotions, and focus our mental fortitude to win the victory. If you want to run faster, throw farther, or jump higher, then you must challenge yourself.

In the same way, if you want to get spiritually fit and experience the promises of God for yourself, then you must challenge yourself to train as an athlete does, but for a far greater reward than any athlete obtains! This book is for people who want to learn to live like God's athletes – as members of God's championship team!

There are three sections in this book to help you accomplish the goal of learning to live like a champion today.

1) **Live Like a Champion Today!** This first section lays the foundation for this book. The two chapters in Section 1 are short and accessible on purpose and give you the information you need to be successful in this challenge.

2) **The 40 Promises in 40 Days Challenge!** It's game time! The second section is composed of 40 short devotionals on 40 promises of God that you will be directed to meditate upon, one per day, for 40 days. The goal of these focused meditations is for you to cultivate the mindset of an athlete – God's athlete! While each devotion is written so that you can read it in less than five minutes, the challenge is for you to apply each one directly to your life all day long and internalize each of the promises of God deep into your mind and heart so that you can run the right play at the right time. God's athletes must learn to listen to the Coach's (God's) voice as He directs the team to play like champions together. Athletes are encouraged to utilize the provided memory cards in the Appendix in order to accomplish this challenge.

3) **The Precious and Magnificent Promises of God!** The third section provides a more thorough biblical and theological

framework for this challenge, and its effectiveness in our lives through a study of 2 Peter 1. All athletes will benefit from this deeper study of God's Word as you learn how to live like a champion today, beyond the scope of the 40-Day Challenge. This section equips you to be able to read your Bible like a champion and be able to apply every promise of God to your everyday life.

Through this book, and the 40-Day Challenge, you are invited to develop and demonstrate the discipline of an athlete and live like a champion today! This is who you were designed to be and have been saved to become. This is the life the Holy Spirit empowers you to live – as a member of God's championship team! As the Apostle Paul says about God's team in Romans 8:37, "But in all these things we overwhelmingly conquer through Him who loved us."

You are a champion in Christ Jesus; therefore, live like a champion today!

Dr. Jerry D. Ingalls

SECTION 1

LIVE LIKE A CHAMPION TODAY!

The star performer himself didn't achieve his excellence by trying to behave a certain way only during the game. Instead, he chose an overall life of preparation of mind and body pouring all his energies into that total preparation, to provide a foundation in the body's automatic responses and strength for his conscious efforts during the game. … And what is true of specific activities is, of course, also true of life as a whole. … A baseball player who expects to excel in the game without adequate exercise in his body is no more ridiculous than the Christian who hopes to be able to act in the manner of Christ when put to the test without the appropriate exercise in godly living. As is obvious from the record of his own life, Jesus understood this fact well and lived accordingly. … To live as Christ lived is to live as he did all his life.[2]

2 Dallas Willard, *The Spirit of the Disciplines: Understanding How God Changes Lives* (New York, NY: HarperCollins, 1988), 3-5.

Dr. Jerry D. Ingalls

Chapter 1
Champions Know Devotion

Every athlete wants to be a champion, but only champions have learned what it is to live a life of devotion! I know, because, once upon a time, I was an accomplished athlete.

I have made it my greatest ambition to live as an athlete for God beyond my glory days as a track and field athlete in the weight and hammer throw events at the United States Military Academy at West Point, and as a member of the United States Army's World Class Athlete Program. A quarter of a century later I still hold the Academy's record and the Patriot League's record in the hammer throw, both set in 1996. After earning many accolades as an All-American athlete and first team Academic All-American, I went on to compete at the highest national level of my sport, earning two berths to the USA Track and Field Olympic Team Trials in the hammer throw (1996 and 2000) with the highest finish of fourth place in my final 2000 effort, narrowly missing the team in an exciting final round of competition. I'll tell you that story in the conclusion of this book. In 1999, I was a member of Team USA for the World University Games in Spain and the US Armed Forces Team for the World Military Games in Croatia.

Those were the days ...

The days of discipline! To be a champion I had to devote myself to the task at hand, day in and day out. Whether that was preparing to beat Navy, winning a Patriot League title, or competing for a spot on the Olympic Team, I had to focus myself daily to be at my best and bring home the prize! I learned from personal experience that the road to breaking records that stand for over a quarter of a century, being selected as a first-team Academic All-American, or being chosen for a national team to represent our great country on the international stage does not happen by accident. It is a life of dedication, sacrifice, and focus!

Those glory days of athletics taught me how to live a life of devotion. While those accomplishments are now over two decades old, I continue to apply the lessons learned to my life as God's athlete in my daily walk with Jesus as His yokefellow and as a member of His body in my local church community. I've learned something over the last twenty years about what is worth my devotion and what is not. After narrowly missing the Olympic Team in 2000, I had set my eyes on the 2004 USA Track and Field Olympic Team Trials for one last effort, but in 2003 I resigned from my sport and entered seminary. I was overwhelmed by a higher calling! Nineteen years later, I have no regrets in this major shift in my life of devotion and, by God's grace, and just for fun this time, I have won a couple masters track and field national titles (2016 & 2017).

I have always been a man committed to living a life of devotion! Along the way and over the years, I've learned to be careful about where I invest my devotion, because people are shaped by their devotion. We reflect that which we serve! In fact, God designed us to be shaped by our devotions because it is His will that we be shaped by Him and into the image of His Son Jesus Christ through a daily yokefellow life with Jesus Christ. I believe this is why dedication to a sport is so appealing to so many of us. We are designed by God to dedicate our lives wholly and to live like a champion. For so many, sports have been their means to do just that. God has a better plan!

The application of athletics to following Jesus is not a new concept. While we have no historical evidence that the Apostle Paul was an athlete, we have plenty of evidence that Paul used athletic imagery to help his hearers understand the life of following Jesus Christ. Take a moment to read six examples from Paul, with one additional example from the author of Hebrews, giving us seven New Testament examples of how the devotion of an athlete applies to being a follower of Jesus:

1. **1 Corinthians 9:24-27.** "Do you not know that those who run in a race all run, but only one receives the prize? Run in such a way that you may win. Everyone who competes in the games exercises self-control in all things. They then do it to receive a perishable wreath, but we an imperishable. Therefore I run in such a way, as not without aim; I box in such a way, as not beating the air; but I discipline my body and make it my slave, so that, after I have preached to others, I myself will not be disqualified."

2. **Philippians 2:14-16.** "Do all things without grumbling or disputing; so that you will prove yourselves to be blameless and innocent, children of God above reproach in the midst of a crooked and perverse generation, among whom you appear as lights in the world, holding fast the word of life, so that in the day of Christ I will have reason to glory because I did not run in vain nor toil in vain."

3. **Galatians 2:2.** "It was because of a revelation that I went up; and I submitted to them the gospel which I preach among the Gentiles, but I did so in private to those who were of reputation, for fear that I might be running, or had run, in vain."

9

4. **Galatians 5:7.** "You were running well; who hindered you from obeying the truth?"

5. **2 Timothy 2:5.** "Also if anyone competes as an athlete, he does not win the prize unless he competes according to the rules."

6. **2 Timothy 4:7-8.** "I have fought the good fight, I have finished the course, I have kept the faith; in the future there is laid up for me the crown of righteousness, which the Lord, the righteous Judge, will award to me on that day; and not only to me, but also to all who have loved His appearing."

7. **Hebrews 12:1-3.** "Therefore, since we have so great a cloud of witnesses surrounding us, let us also lay aside every encumbrance and the sin which so easily entangles us, and let us run with endurance the race that is set before us, fixing our eyes on Jesus, the author and perfecter of faith, who for the joy set before Him endured the cross, despising the shame, and has sat down at the right hand of the throne of God. For consider Him who has endured such hostility by sinners against Himself, so that you will not grow weary and lose heart."

The New Testament witness demonstrates that athletes were known for their life of devotion. Paul alludes to the ancient Olympic sports of running and boxing. He compares the life of following Jesus to the rigors not only of competing, but of the focus required to discipline oneself to train and be ready for the games and compete in such a way as not to be disqualified. Followers of Jesus must be wholly committed to winning the prize – the life of a champion!

Paul clearly has a high view of athletes and their life of devotion to sport and the goal of winning the prize, but Paul also makes it very clear that there is a higher calling to a person's life of devotion. He says to his protégé in 1 Timothy 4:7b-8, "On the other hand, discipline yourself for the purpose of godliness; for bodily discipline is only of little profit, but godliness is profitable for all things, since it holds promise for the present life and also for the life to come."

What are the promises of godliness for this present life, and for eternal life to come, that are of greater profit than the discipline of athletes to train and prepare their bodies for sport and its short-lived victories? What does it mean to discipline yourself for the purpose of godliness and how do we do that on a day-to-day basis?

This book seeks to answer these questions and give you a winning game plan on how to live like a champion today. We now turn to that winning game plan in Chapter 2.

Chapter 2
Champions Need a Winning Game Plan

We all know that for a team to win the championship, every athlete must play the game like a champion! The winning game plan calls for each member of the team to do the following so that the team can experience the victory:

1) Know the team's playbook.
2) Train to be in great shape.
3) Listen to the coach.
4) Work together with the other players as one team.

These are the four action steps of the winning game plan that will be drilled into us throughout this book as we learn the precious and magnificent promises of God. Through the promises of God, we become partakers of the divine nature to the glory of God, as Peter so clearly explains in 2 Peter 1:2-4:

Grace and peace be multiplied to you in the knowledge of God and of Jesus our Lord; seeing that His divine power has granted to us everything pertaining to life and godliness, through the true knowledge of Him who called us by His own glory and excellence. For by these He has granted to us His precious and magnificent promises, so that by them you may become partakers of the divine nature, having escaped the corruption that is in the world by lust.[3]

---

3 If you are interested in a detailed study of 2 Peter 1 that lays the biblical framework for this book and the winning game plan, then read Section 3.

As athletes of God, we are invited to learn what the precious and magnificent promises of God are so that we "may become partakers of the divine nature" to the glory of God. This is not an intellectual exercise, but a practical one as members of God's team; therefore, we must also do those same action steps if we are to live like a champion today:

1) Know God's playbook – the Bible – by learning the promises of God.

2) Train ourselves for godliness by learning to live according to the promises of God.

3) Learn how to listen to the Coach's (God's) voice so that we run the right play at the right time.

4) Work together as members of God's team – His Church.

Action Step #1: Know God's Playbook

We are members of God's team, and we need to know God's playbook to run the right plays at the right time. God has given us everything we need to do His will for His glory.

Paul exhorts his protégé in 2 Timothy 3:16-17, "All Scripture is inspired by God and profitable for teaching, for reproof, for correction, for training in righteousness; so that the [athlete] of God may be adequate, equipped for every good work."

Do you know the promises of God?

The promises of God are found in the Bible (God's playbook), and they are your way of experiencing and living in the victory of Jesus Christ, which He accomplished through His finished work on the Cross. Throughout this book, we will be learning to meditate upon the promises of God by internalizing them, or hiding them in our hearts, just as Psalm 119:11 states, "Your word I have treasured in my heart, that I may not sin against You." Memory Cards are provided for you in the Appendix to assist you in this important action step of the winning game plan.

God promises a great reward for those who train themselves according to this discipline of memorizing His promises. Joshua 1:8 declares, "This book of the law shall not depart from your mouth, but you shall meditate on it day and night, so that you may be careful to do according to all that is written in it; for then you will make your way prosperous, and then you will have success." The promises of God are the way to victory in every area of your life!

Action Step #2: Train Ourselves for Godliness

We are God's athletes, and we need to exercise our faith to win the victory! We are called to train ourselves for godliness and to be ready at any time to run God's play! Paul teaches this in 1 Timothy 4:7b-10 (ESV):

> Rather train yourself for godliness; for while bodily training is of some value, godliness is of value in every way, as it holds promise for the present life and also for the life to come. The saying is trustworthy and deserving of full acceptance. For to this end we toil and strive, because we have our hope set on the living God, who is the Savior of all people, especially of those who believe.

Are you in spiritual training?

I can testify to you that physical training does have a season of glory, and I can attest that, whether that season ends in high school, in college, or at the highest level of the sport, one day, even for the most celebrated of athletes, those glory days will come to an end. What then do you have left and how have you been formed by your life of devotion? Who have you become in the pursuit of athletic glory and who are you on the other side of it?

The good news is that when we train ourselves in godliness, the fullness of the victory is always yet to come. The glory days are never behind us, but always before us. When we train ourselves according to the Word of God, the living God sets before us a future that has the truest and highest honor of being welcomed into the "Victor's Circle" of Heaven. Paul states this in 1 Corinthians 9:24-27:

Do you not know that those who run in a race all run, but only one receives the prize? Run in such a way that you may win. Everyone who competes in the games exercises self-control in all things. They then do it to receive a perishable wreath, but we an imperishable. Therefore I run in such a way, as not without aim; I box in such a way, as not beating the air; but I discipline my body and make it my slave, so that, after I have preached to others, I myself will not be disqualified.

The life of devotion is an essential part of experiencing the victory of God in your daily life.

Action Step #3: Listen to the Coach

We are God's athletes, so that makes God our Coach; therefore, we need to learn the Coach's voice so we can play the right play at the right time! When the Coach calls us into the game, we must be ready to obey, even if we don't understand exactly what the Coach is thinking. We cultivate the mindset of trusting that God is good and has a victorious purpose in mind for all that He commands. Jesus explains the importance of knowing the Coach's voice in John 10:3-5, 10b:

> But he who enters by the door is a shepherd [coach] of the sheep [athletes]. To him the doorkeeper opens, and the sheep hear his voice, and he calls his own sheep by name and leads them out. When he puts forth all his own, he goes ahead of them, and the sheep follow him because they know his voice. A stranger they simply will not follow, but will flee from him, because they do not know the voice of strangers. ... I came that they may have life, and have it abundantly.

Do you know the Coach's voice and trust Him so well that you respond without hesitation?

Jesus promises that His victory will bring the "abundant" life – a fullness of life that can only come through your fellowship in His Trinity – the Godhead of Father, Son, and Holy Spirit. Now, let's be clear, the victory I am calling us to live, and the championship I am calling us to win, is not always our health and wealth, or our worldly success and prosperity. But it is always right and true because it is a part of God's good plans!

The abundant life that God promises through Jesus Christ is the fullness of His presence – your partaking of His divine nature. It is only then that we can have the fullness of joy, the sufficiency of grace, the perfection of love, or the rest for our soul that comes through His peace guarding our hearts and minds in Christ Jesus.

The abundant life is exactly what Paul promises every believer in Romans 8:29-32:

For those whom He foreknew, He also predestined to become conformed to the image of His Son, so that He would be the firstborn among many brethren; and these whom He predestined, He also called; and these whom He called, He also justified; and these whom He justified, He also glorified. What then shall we say to these things? If God is for us, who is against us? He who did not spare His own Son, but delivered Him over for us all, how will He not also with Him freely give us all things?

In learning to trust the Coach and listen for His voice in times of meditation upon His promises, and through mindfulness of His presence throughout the day, we become sensitized to the plans of God. We begin to see the big picture of how His ultimate purpose in all things is our conformity to Christ and His glory. God invites us to listen for His voice to partner with Him in this victory!

Action Step #4: Work Together as Members of God's Team

We are God's team, and the victory we live is God's victory! The championship celebration is guaranteed; we are invited to live like champions, as one team, today, knowing the victory is already ours in Christ

Jesus! Paul explains to us in Romans 8:37-39:

> But in all these things we overwhelmingly conquer through Him who loved us. For I am convinced that neither death, nor life, nor angels, nor principalities, nor things present, nor things to come, nor powers, nor height, nor depth, nor any other created thing, will be able to separate us from the love of God, which is in Christ Jesus our Lord.

Do you trust and live like God's victory is secure for you, as a member of His body – His church?

Paul teaches us that we are members of the one body of Christ – God's Team! In Romans 12:4-6a, Paul commands us to do our part as members of God's Team:

> For just as we have many members in one body and all the members do not have the same function, so we, who are many, are one body in Christ, and individually members one of another. Since we have gifts that differ according to the grace given to us, each of us is to exercise them accordingly.

This is our way forward; this is the game plan for learning to live like a champion today! Do your part as a member of God's team by learning God's playbook, training yourself for godliness so that you are in good enough shape to run the right play at the right time when the Coach commands, and working together with the other members of the team by prioritizing being a healthy, functional team member. The team must win together; the victory cannot be individual, but it takes the individual members of the team to do their part and work together!

The Invitation: Learn to Live Like a Champion Today

I invite you on a journey through this book. No matter what may come in the circumstances of your life, God is inviting you to live like a champion today by partaking of His divine nature. Jesus is your victory, and He has given you the precious and magnificent promises of God so that you may learn to live with Him – in His victory!

Dr. Jerry D. Ingalls

SECTION 2

THE 40 PROMISES IN 40 DAYS CHALLENGE!

The grace of God is gloriously beyond our skill and technique. The means of grace are not about earning God's favor, twisting his arm, or controlling his blessing, but readying ourselves for consistent saturation in the roll of his tides. Yes, it is grace, and yes, we expend effort. And so the apostle Paul says to his protégé, "Train yourself for godliness" (1 Tim. 4:7). Discipline yourself for growth. Take regular action to get more of God in your mind and your heart, and echo his ways in your life – which will make you increasingly like him ("godliness"). It's a gift, and we receive it as we become it.[4]

---

4 David Mathis, *Habits of Grace: Enjoying Jesus Through the Spiritual Disciplines* (Wheaton, IL: Crossway, 2016), 21, 27-28.

Day 1 Promise 1
The Promise of Grace

1) Know God's Playbook. The play of the day is 2 Corinthians 12:9:

"And [Jesus] has said to me, 'My grace is sufficient for you, for power is perfected in weakness.' Most gladly, therefore, I will rather boast about my weaknesses, so that the power of Christ may dwell in me."

2) Train for Godliness. Grace is the essential power source of the Christian life; it is the "divine power" of our becoming "partakers of the divine nature" (2 Peter 1:2-4). Grace is more than a statement of our status before God (our position on God's team). Grace is how we live out and make visible our salvation (our effectiveness on the playing field).

"For by grace you have been saved through faith; and that not of yourselves, it is the gift of God; not as a result of works, so that no one may boast. For we are His workmanship, created in Christ Jesus for good works, which God prepared beforehand so that we would walk in them" (Ephesians 2:8-10).

An essential part of our training regimen is to know the power source of our Christian life and feed the life of the Spirit through the means of grace: Bible intake, prayer, worship, fellowship, Bible study with other believers, and active participation in the life of a local church. These are just a few of the primary spiritual disciplines that put us in the pathway of experiencing and living in God's promise of grace.

3) Listen to the Coach. God empowers your life as His athlete.

"I can do all things through Him who strengthens me" (Philippians 4:13).

Pray for a deepening of this partnership between you and God, because grace is never opposed to your efforts to please God and live for Him. Rather, grace is opposed to merit – you can't earn it! You live it – it's your life with God!

"So then, my beloved, just as you have always obeyed, not as in my presence only, but now much more in my absence, work out your salvation with fear and trembling; for it is God who is at work in you, both to will and to work for His good pleasure"
(Philippians 2:12-13).

4) Work together with God's team. When I was one of the captains of the Army Track & Field Team at West Point, it was always my desire to see every athlete on the team do their very best. In order to beat Navy and win the Patriot League Championship, which we did, we had to do it as one team!

"To be specific, that the Gentiles are fellow heirs and fellow members of the body, and fellow partakers of the promise in Christ Jesus through the gospel, of which I was made a minister, according to the gift of God's grace which was given to me according to the working of His power" (Ephesians 3:6-7).

Living in grace requires humility from each member of God's team. We must be willing to work hard, yet know that it is God who accomplishes the victory in and through each member of the team.

"For this reason I bow my knees before the Father, from whom every family in heaven and on earth derives its name, that He would grant you, according to the riches of His glory, to be strengthened with power through His Spirit in the inner man, so that Christ may dwell in your hearts through faith; and that you, being rooted and grounded in love, may be able to comprehend with all the saints what is the breadth and length and height and depth, and to know the love of Christ which surpasses knowledge, that you may be filled up to all the fullness of God" (Ephesians 3:14-19).

Living in the promise of grace is how we experience our union with God, and how His power flows through our lives to demonstrate His love to the world! Therefore, run the race faithfully today and execute the play of the day for the glory of God.

Day 2 Promise 2
The Promise of Resurrection and Life

1) Know God's Playbook. The play of the day is John 11:25-26:

"Jesus said to her, 'I am the resurrection and the life; he who believes in Me will live even if he dies, and everyone who lives and believes in Me will never die. Do you believe this?'"

2) Train for Godliness. The resurrection of Jesus Christ is our hope, not only for eternal life, but for today. I like to say that hope is my *superpower* because hope never disappoints (Romans 5:5). I have had periods of hopelessness, as an athlete and as a Christian, and those seasons can be dark and dangerous. It is critical to train the hope of the resurrection into your bones. It's not enough to know about it; you must believe and trust it with every ounce of your being, as if your very life depended on it.

"This hope we have as an anchor of the soul, a hope both sure and steadfast and one which enters within the veil" (Hebrews 6:19).

Hope is not wishful thinking – it is the certainty of the resurrection and life of Jesus Christ, which provides you stability during the trials and tribulations of today. The victory has been won, and bestowed upon you, through faith in Jesus Christ!

"But now Christ has been raised from the dead, the first fruits of those who are asleep. For since by a man came death, by a man also came the resurrection of the dead. For as in Adam all die, so also in Christ all will be made alive" (1 Corinthians 15:20-22).

3) Listen to the Coach. You are alive because He lives! Jesus says that this sin-sick world is not to end in death, but all things will be made new for the glory of God.

"'Behold, the tabernacle of God is among men, and He will dwell among them, and they shall be His people, and God Himself will be among them, and He will wipe away every tear from their eyes; and

there will no longer be any death; there will no longer be any mourning, or crying, or pain; the first things have passed away.' And He who sits on the throne said, 'Behold, I am making all things new.' And He said, 'Write, for these words are faithful and true'" (Revelation 21:3-5).

We are to believe our own Easter story – Jesus is making all things new! Every person needs God's grace and truth. God's game plan is to unbind the captives, set free the oppressed, give sight to the blind, and preach the gospel in word and deed. Run the right play at the right time, "unbind [them], and let [them] go," just as God, in Christ Jesus, set you free (John 11:44; John 8:36)!

4) Work together with God's team. The athletes of God are to encourage and embolden one another with the hope of the resurrection!

"But we do not want you to be uninformed, brethren, about those who are asleep, so that you will not grieve as do the rest who have no hope. For if we believe that Jesus died and rose again, even so God will bring with Him those who have fallen asleep in Jesus. For this we say to you by the word of the Lord, that we who are alive and remain until the coming of the Lord, will not precede those who have fallen asleep. ... Therefore comfort one another with these words" (1 Thessalonians 4:13-15, 18).

We all need courage and comfort in these dark days. The resurrection of Jesus Christ, just like the final victory revealed to us in the New Heaven and New Earth, is given to us to give us hope when hope feels forlorn. Have courage, and face your day, knowing the victory is won – there is hope! Therefore, run the race faithfully today and execute the play of the day for the glory of God.

Day 3 Promise 3
The Promise of the Holy Spirit

1) Know God's Playbook. The play of the day is John 14:26:

"But the Helper, the Holy Spirit, whom the Father will send in My name, He will teach you all things, and bring to your remembrance all that I said to you."

2) Train for Godliness. This promise is the power source for living like a champion today! The athletes of God do not need performance enhancing drugs, or any other such cheat, to win the victory. You have the Spirit of the Living God, the resurrection power of God, living in you.

"You are from God, little children, and have overcome them; because greater is He who is in you than he who is in the world" (1 John 4:4).

We train in this promise by hearing the invitation to walk in the Spirit and not by the flesh. The promise of the Holy Spirit not only secures our victory by the eternal presence of God living in us, but the Holy Spirit also empowers us to live like champions today!

"But I say, walk by the Spirit, and you will not carry out the desire of the flesh. For the flesh sets its desire against the Spirit, and the Spirit against the flesh; for these are in opposition to one another, so that you may not do the things that you please. But if you are led by the Spirit, you are not under the Law. ... But the fruit of the Spirit is love, joy, peace, patience, kindness, goodness, faithfulness, gentleness, self-control; against such things there is no law. Now those who belong to Christ Jesus have crucified the flesh with its passions and desires. If we live by the Spirit, let us also walk by the Spirit" (Galatians 5:16-25).

3) Listen to the Coach. Jesus gave His followers clear teaching on the necessity of the Holy Spirit to live like a champion today. This was the purpose for the first Pentecost.

"Gathering them together, [Jesus] commanded them not to leave Jerusalem, but to wait for what the Father had promised, 'Which,' He

said, 'you heard of from Me; for John baptized with water, but you will be baptized with the Holy Spirit not many days from now'" (Acts 1:4-5).

This is not the first time the followers of Jesus heard this invitation to be baptized in the Spirit, because the baptism of the Spirit is the very nature of salvation itself – the Spirit of God is our inheritance. The presence and power of God dwelling in us, the Giver of new life transforming us into a temple of the Holy Spirit and inviting us into the eternal fellowship of Father, Son, and Holy Spirit by allowing us to participate in His divine nature, is what it means to have salvation. The Son removed our sins from us through His sacrificial death on the Cross so that God could live in us through His Spirit!

"Do you not know that your body is a temple of the Holy Spirit who is in you, whom you have from God, and that you are not your own? For you have been bought with a price: therefore glorify God in your body" (1 Corinthians 6:19-20).

4) Work together with God's team. God is with us! God will never leave us! These are the good fruits of the promise of the Holy Spirit. God is ours in His fullness and brings fullness to our lives – the victorious life!

"This Jesus God raised up again, to which we are all witnesses. Therefore having been exalted to the right hand of God, and having received from the Father the promise of the Holy Spirit, He has poured forth this which you both see and hear" (Acts 2:32-33).

God is with us through His presence and power living in us! May God be exalted in and through His Church! Therefore, run the race faithfully today and execute the play of the day for the glory of God.

Day 4 Promise 4
The Promise of Gathering

1) Know God's Playbook. The play of the day is Hebrews 10:24-25:

"Let us consider how to stimulate one another to love and good deeds, not forsaking our own assembling together, as is the habit of some, but encouraging one another; and all the more as you see the day drawing near."

2) Train for Godliness. Jesus is the One who gathers us – He calls us out by name! We gather in obedience to Jesus because it has always been, and always will be, His idea and not our own. We are designed to portray the image of God (Genesis 1:27) and to shine His light for His glory; we do that best, together, as the one body of Christ!

"There is one body and one Spirit, just as also you were called in one hope of your calling; one Lord, one faith, one baptism, one God and Father of all who is over all and through all and in all" (Ephesians 4:4-6).

"You are the light of the world. A city set on a hill cannot be hidden; nor does anyone light a lamp and put it under a basket, but on the lampstand, and it gives light to all who are in the house. Let your light shine before men in such a way that they may see your good works, and glorify your Father who is in heaven" (Matthew 5:14-16).

God requires His athletes to show up for practice, and pay attention at team meetings, so that they know how to run the right play, at the right time, together. While you may have a daily training regimen on your own, the Coach wants you to know your teammates, and wants you to grow with them, because living His victory requires teamwork.

3) Listen to the Coach. The promise of gathering requires the habit of prioritizing first things first. Champions know that the life of devotion requires prioritizing their lives around their goal – the victory! No one makes it to the Olympics without this habit; it forms every athlete's schedule and life rhythm.

"But seek first His kingdom and His righteousness, and all these things will be added to you" (Matthew 6:33).

It is my habit to prioritize assembling with God's team, my church family, as an intentional spiritual discipline. It is like prioritizing prayer before meals, or Bible intake before media exposure, or a day of rest once per week. These are the rhythms of grace that you are invited to live in, so that you can live like a champion today.

"Day by day continuing with one mind in the temple, and breaking bread from house to house, they were taking their meals together with gladness and sincerity of heart, praising God and having favor with all the people. And the Lord was adding to their number day by day those who were being saved" (Acts 2:46-47).

4) Work together with God's team. The promise of gathering invites each of us to have a *participant* mentality, not that of a *spectator*! While athletes appreciate being cheered on and supported, it is the participants who memorize the play book, train themselves, listen for the coach's voice, and run the plays as a team. We are inspired and encouraged best by those who are on the playing field with us!

"Let the word of Christ richly dwell within you, with all wisdom teaching and admonishing one another with psalms and hymns and spiritual songs, singing with thankfulness in your hearts to God" (Colossians 3:16).

As you gather as a fellow member of God's team, you are transformed by the renewal of your mind through Spirit-filled times of worship in song, prayer, liturgical practices, and Bible teaching. Prioritize first things first, not just for the once-per-week gathering, but as a rhythm of life throughout your week. Therefore, run the race faithfully today and execute the play of the day for the glory of God.

Day 5 Promise 5
The Promise of Security

1) Know God's Playbook. The play of the day is Romans 8:38-39:

"For I am convinced that neither death, nor life, nor angels, nor principalities, nor things present, nor things to come, nor powers, nor height, nor depth, nor any other created thing, will be able to separate us from the love of God, which is in Christ Jesus our Lord."

2) Train for Godliness. The promise of security was given to us as our assurance of God's work of salvation, which dictates how we live our lives – how we think and feel!

An example of this kind of security is found in the everyday practice of parenting. Whether the child experiences security or insecurity in his or her parents' love will determine and shape the child's ability to trust his or her parents and respond to their discipline and instruction. Parents must intentionally work to cultivate the mindset of trust and heart attitude of security into their child. This takes time and intentional effort; it must be trained!

In God, our security is in the salvation of our souls! God has given us ample evidence and reason to trust Him and be secure in His love. We must train into our minds the right view of God because there is nothing more important about a child of God than what he or she thinks about God! Jesus gave us secure words to meditate upon.

"My sheep hear My voice, and I know them, and they follow Me; and I give eternal life to them, and they will never perish; and no one will snatch them out of My hand. My Father, who has given them to Me, is greater than all; and no one is able to snatch them out of the Father's hand. I and the Father are one" (John 10:27-30).

3) Listen to the Coach. Get to know the character of the God who called and chose you!

In 1999, Coach Jerry Quiller, the 2000 Olympic Coach for Team USA Track & Field, put his name next to my name as a Team USA selection for the World University Games. I was not a favored pick, because I had missed two previous seasons due to military service in the 82nd Airborne Division, but Coach Quiller stood with me. Because of him my spot was secure on the team, and I had my best international competition, representing Team USA proudly.

Every athlete needs to feel secure in the Coach's calling! The athlete's testimony needs to be, "I am a part of this team because the Coach chose me!" This freedom from fear, because of the promise of security, is our great strength as the athletes of God. It yokes us to the Coach, and to one another, in His victory, allowing us to live like champions today.

"There is no fear in love; but perfect love casts out fear, because fear involves punishment, and the one who fears is not perfected in love" (1 John 4:18).

Our assurance grows as we learn to distinguish between God's secure voice and our own insecure voice, between God's perfect love to us and our imperfect love to Him. Spending time in prayer and God's Word trains this into our hearts and minds!

4) Work together with God's team. Security with God is the foundation from which we can cooperate with one another as the body of Christ. Relationships are the evidence of our faith, and they are the hardest work of being a Christian. Ultimately, Christianity is not a life of rules, dos and don'ts, religious activities, or intellectual beliefs; rather, Christianity is a relationship with the God, who *is* love, saving us *through* His love, for the sake of *being* love to the world!

"We love, because He first loved us" (1 John 4:19).

Liberating you to live on mission is the promise of security – you can never lose your place on God's team (Romans 8:1)! Therefore, run the race faithfully today and execute the play of the day for the glory of God.

Day 6 Promise 6
The Promise of a New Beginning

1) Know God's Playbook. The play of the day is 2 Corinthians 5:17:

"Therefore if anyone is in Christ, he is a new creature; the old things passed away; behold, new things have come."

2) Train for Godliness. Even after the worst of days, or seasons, there is a new opportunity set before us every time we are willing to embrace it. When a person responds in faith to the grace of God, the Lord Jesus Christ brings new life, every time, because Jesus' Kingdom is about resurrection power – making all things new (Revelation 21:5)!

This promise is for those who are "in Christ." Are you walking in a personal relationship with Him? Are you experiencing the promise of a new beginning?

"We know that we have passed out of death into life, because we love the brethren. He who does not love abides in death" (1 John 3:14).

You are unwilling to begin a new life when you remain codependent with the old self – you can't keep your old life on life support just in case Jesus doesn't work for you! Paul knew this intimately as a former religious leader. He had to die to religion to be born again to a relationship with God through Jesus Christ.

"I have been crucified with Christ; and it is no longer I who live, but Christ lives in me; and the life which I now live in the flesh I live by faith in the Son of God, who loved me and gave Himself up for me" (Galatians 2:20).

You can't live the old life and experience the promise of a new beginning at the same time, because beauty comes from ashes – that's the promise of Isaiah 61:3! What do you need to lay down at the Cross in order to experience a new beginning?

3) Listen to the Coach. You can experience satisfaction and joy in your relationship with God by trusting Him daily for the promise of a new beginning. You can feel accomplished and successful in Christ alone. You can know who you are and have purpose in your life. This is what Christ has done for you and the ministry He has given you!

"Now all these things are from God, who reconciled us to Himself through Christ and gave us the ministry of reconciliation, namely, that God was in Christ reconciling the world to Himself, not counting their trespasses against them, and He has committed to us the word of reconciliation. Therefore, we are ambassadors for Christ, as though God were making an appeal through us; we beg you on behalf of Christ, be reconciled to God" (2 Corinthians 5:18-20).

Are you believing God for His promise of a new beginning? If not, I beg you to be reconciled to God through a personal relationship with Jesus Christ.

4) Work together with God's team. When you are "in Christ," you are a signpost of the New Heaven and New Earth! You are already a new creation, reconciled to God through the crucifixion and resurrection of Jesus Christ. Forget the old life, the corruption of the world from which you have escaped, and put on the new life Christ has given you as a partaker of His divine nature (2 Peter 1:4)!

"But one thing I do: forgetting what lies behind and reaching forward to what lies ahead, I press on toward the goal for the prize of the upward call of God in Christ Jesus" (Philippians 3:13b-14).

We are a new creation, chosen by God, reconciled by the Son and empowered by the Holy Spirit, compelled by His love to go in grace as His ambassadors, signposts of the new creation! Therefore, run the race faithfully today and execute the play of the day for the glory of God.

Day 7 Promise 7
The Promise of Faith

1) Know God's Playbook. The play of the day is Romans 12:3:

"For through the grace given to me I say to everyone among you not to think more highly of himself than he ought to think; but to think so as to have sound judgment, as God has allotted to each a measure of faith."

2) Train for Godliness. When God's athletes understand where their abilities come from, they honor God with their athletic abilities rather than themselves! God receives all the glory when His athletes have been humbled by the promise of faith!

"The assurance of things hoped for, the conviction of things not seen. For by it the men of old gained approval. By faith we understand that the worlds were prepared by the word of God, so that what is seen was not made out of things which are visible" (Hebrews 11:1-3).

We cannot take for granted the gift of faith, assuming it will grow simply because we made a profession of faith. That would be "thinking more highly" than we ought of ourselves. In using sound judgment, we create an environment full of spiritual friendships and disciplines that become a "trellis" on which our branch grows in union with the Vine and bears much fruit!

3) Listen to the Coach. The "trellis" is like an athlete's training regimen – it focuses the athlete's efforts for maximum effectiveness and fruitfulness! It is the image of the ancient church practice of having a "rule of life" – not "rules," but "a rule," – a trellis of life.

"Abide in Me, and I in you. As the branch cannot bear fruit of itself unless it abides in the vine, so neither can you unless you abide in Me. I am the vine, you are the branches; he who abides in Me and I

**in him, he bears much fruit, for apart from Me
you can do nothing" (John 15:4-5).**

By prioritizing the spiritual disciplines of abiding in Jesus as a part of your daily training regimen as God's athlete, your faith becomes a conduit of the power of God – flowing from the throne of Heaven to and through you. The Holy Spirit flows through the vine of union with Jesus Christ and moves your faith from a theoretical concept to an everyday fruit-bearing reality.

"But the fruit of the Spirit is love, joy, peace, patience, kindness, goodness, faithfulness, gentleness, self-control; against such things there is no law. Now those who belong to Christ Jesus have crucified the flesh with its passions and desires. If we live by the Spirit, let us also walk by the Spirit" (Galatians 5:22-25).

4) Work together with God's team. While we are saved by faith alone, faith never stands alone! You are not a solitary person, facing the world and all its problems alone. You are a member of a team that is making God's victory manifest in the world for many to come and see that God is good and that His Kingdom is righteous and true!

"The kingdom of heaven is like a mustard seed, which a man took and sowed in his field; and this is smaller than all other seeds, but when it is full grown, it is larger than the garden plants and becomes a tree, so that the birds of the air come and nest in its branches" (Matthew 13:31-32).

As a member of God's team, you learn from the Coach that "without faith it is impossible to please Him" (Hebrews 11:6)! Therefore, run the race faithfully today and execute the play of the day for the glory of God.

Day 8 Promise 8
The Promise of Membership

1) Know God's Playbook. The play of the day is Romans 12:4-5:

"For just as we have many members in one body and all the members do not have the same function, so we, who are many, are one body in Christ, and individually members one of another."

2) Train for Godliness. You are an essential piece of a living organism, and we, the Church of Jesus Christ, are only as healthy as each of our individual parts. This is the imagery of God's team from God's Word! God intends us to be a mutually dependent people, created in His image of community (Father, Son, and Holy Spirit).

Paul very intentionally gave us the body imagery of membership so that we can understand just how important the promise of membership is, not only to us as the individuals, but to the whole living organism of the Church. We are completely dependent on Jesus, the head of the Church, for our life, and we are mutually dependent on one another, the fellow members of Christ's body, for our effectiveness. This entire promise is a call to teamwork on God's team!

"For the body is not one member, but many. If the foot says, 'Because I am not a hand, I am not a part of the body,' it is not for this reason any the less a part of the body. And if the ear says, 'Because I am not an eye, I am not a part of the body,' it is not for this reason any the less a part of the body. If the whole body were an eye, where would the hearing be? If the whole were hearing, where would the sense of smell be? But now God has placed the members, each one of them, in the body, just as He desired. If they were all one member, where would the body be? But now there are many members, but one body" (1 Corinthians 12:14-20).

3) Listen to the Coach. Membership is a privilege that comes with responsibilities. The health and growth of the body of Christ is intimately yoked with you and your experience of a life-giving faith. You are invited to walk together with the other members of your local church and watch what

God will do in and through His body. Jesus Christ is the only head to which we all, leader and member alike, must submit.

"And He put all things in subjection under His feet, and gave Him as head over all things to the church, which is His body, the fullness of Him who fills all in all" (Ephesians 1:22-23; cf. Colossians 1:18).

4) Work together with God's team. It is the work of the Holy Spirit to fulfill the promise of membership, and it is Jesus who gives some to be spiritual leaders who are called to equip the body of Christ to walk in the maturity of their faith in Him (Ephesians 4:11-12).

"Speaking the truth in love, we are to grow up in all aspects into Him who is the head, even Christ, from whom the whole body, being fitted and held together by what every joint supplies, according to the proper working of each individual part, causes the growth of the body for the building up of itself in love" (Ephesians 4:15-16).

"There is one body and one Spirit, just as also you were called in one hope of your calling; one Lord, one faith, one baptism, one God and Father of all who is over all and through all and in all" (Ephesians 4:4-6).

Submit yourself to the work of the Holy Spirit so that you will be a healthy, functional member of the one body of Christ in your local congregation. This invitation is for every person on the team, whether as a member or a leader, to do his or her part! We are in this together! Therefore, run the race faithfully today and execute the play of the day for the glory of God.

Day 9 Promise 9
The Promise of Adoption

1) Know God's Playbook. The play of the day is Romans 8:15:

"For you have not received a spirit of slavery leading to fear again, but you have received a spirit of adoption as sons by which we cry out, 'Abba! Father!'"

2) Train for Godliness. Just like a highly prized athlete has a legal contract signed for them to be a part of a professional team, so God purchases us for His team through His Son's blood.

Adoption is the Holy Spirit's ministry of the Father's grace towards His lost children through the provision of His Son Jesus Christ. Jesus came so that all the sons and daughters could be bought back from the penalty of sin, for the wages of sin is death, and brought Home to God's forever family. Jesus's blood is the satisfaction of God's judgment for sin (1 John 2:2; 4:9-10). This is how you become a member of God's team, through a legal transaction; you have been bought at a price – you are a highly valued athlete! Train this truth into your heart and mind!

"Or do you not know that your body is a temple of the Holy Spirit who is in you, whom you have from God, and that you are not your own? For you have been bought with a price: therefore glorify God in your body" (1 Corinthians 6:20).

3) Listen to the Coach. Adoption is a part of God's plan of salvation to redeem all things back to His rightful rule, which the Bible calls the Kingdom of God; this plan is often taught through the imagery of a family ("familial imagery"). Like a loving parent, God wants all His children to come home (Luke 15:11-32)!

Until the Lord returns, this is our purpose as the children of God – the sons and daughters of the King of kings – with rights of inheritance to His presence, His power, and His promises! Therefore, there is no reason to fear; you are no longer a slave to fear, but a "son of God" (Romans 8:14-25). You are a child of God with legal rights of inheritance to Jesus' victory!

"But when the fullness of the time came, God sent forth His Son, born of a woman, born under the Law, so that He might redeem those who were under the Law, that we might receive the adoption as sons. Because you are sons, God has sent forth the Spirit of His Son into our hearts, crying, 'Abba! Father!' Therefore you are no longer a slave, but a son; and if a son, then an heir through God"
(Galatians 4:4-7).

4) Work together with God's team. The Holy Spirit assures you of God's grace in your life, forever. Because of the plan of the Father, the provision of the Son, and the promise of the Holy Spirit, you do not get what you deserve, but rather you receive grace upon grace through the ministry of adoption. Rather than being cast aside because of the sin that separates us from our heavenly Father, we are welcomed into His large, forever family with lots of brothers and sisters.

"For you are all sons of God through faith in Christ Jesus. For all of you who were baptized into Christ have clothed yourselves with Christ. There is neither Jew nor Greek, there is neither slave nor free man, there is neither male nor female; for you are all one in Christ Jesus" (Galatians 3:26-27).

Our witness as the children of God is how we live our lives with God, and with one another, as His family, in Christian unity. Our lives are the signs and wonders of the Kingdom of God! This is the promise of adoption for all to see and know that there is a God who loves all the little children. Therefore, run the race faithfully today and execute the play of the day for the glory of God.

Day 10 Promise 10
The Promise of Following Jesus

1) Know God's Playbook. The play of the day is Mark 1:17:

"And Jesus said to them, 'Follow Me, and I will make you become fishers of men.'"

2) Train for Godliness. When I was training for the Olympics, I watched a lot of videos and studied a lot of still frames of world class hammer throwers. I studied their techniques and learned from their training regimens. I did this so I could be the very best hammer thrower I could be. Jesus calls us to do the same with Him for life and godliness – to follow His teaching and way of life so that we can be the very best version of ourselves to the glory of God!

Our responsibility in the Christian life is to listen for the call of Jesus to "Follow Me" and then respond with integrity. Our response doesn't begin and end with that one-time event, but continues as a moment-by-moment lifestyle. Jesus' invitation to "Follow Me" connects to an important Hebrew word, הלך (*hālakh*). For the Jewish people, *hālakh* took on the meaning of habitually practicing, or walking in a certain lifestyle, as the way of fulfilling God's invitation of covenant relationship.

"Come, let us go up to the mountain of the LORD, to the house of the God of Jacob; that He may teach us concerning His ways and that we may walk in His paths" (Isaiah 2:3).

The training regimen of following Jesus is to take on yourself the *hālakh* or "habitual practice" of His way of life – walk His walk and talk His talk. Jesus was being very intentional in His invitation because He knew that His way of life was the only way to please God.

"Jesus said to him, 'I am the way, and the truth, and the life; no one comes to the Father but through Me'" (John 14:6).

3) Listen to the Coach. The results are guaranteed for all who accept the invitation. Jesus promised, "I will make you become fishers of people." In other words, Jesus is promising that God will not only choose you to be on His team, but the Holy Spirit will call upon you to get in the game and run the right play at the right time. Your responsibility is to study Jesus so that you are ready to be effectively used by God at any moment of any day.

"For by these He has granted to us His precious and magnificent promises, so that by them you may become partakers of the divine nature, having escaped the corruption that is in the world by lust" (2 Peter 1:4).

Studying Jesus requires each of us to study the life of Jesus Christ from the Gospel accounts of Matthew, Mark, Luke, and John. Just like I studied videos and still frame photos to learn from the very best, the athletes of God must study the life and ministry of Jesus to be their very best.

4) Work together with God's team. Following Jesus is the way of victory for God's team; in working together, we demonstrate the glory of God in our coordinated efforts.

"The glory which You have given Me I have given to them, that they may be one, just as We are one; I in them and You in Me, that they may be perfected in unity, so that the world may know that You sent Me, and loved them, even as You have loved Me" (John 17:22-23).

Jesus' invitation to salvation, "Follow Me," comes with everything you need for life and godliness, wholeness and holiness. It includes your call not only to become like Him, but to partner with Him and His team in the mission of God. There is only one invitation, one calling, and it is for each of us to answer. It is our continual response to the invitation to follow Jesus that unites us as one team. Therefore, run the race faithfully today and execute the play of the day for the glory of God.

Day 11 Promise 11
The Promise of a Seal

1) Know God's Playbook. The play of the day is Ephesians 1:13-14:

"In Him, you also, after listening to the message of truth, the gospel of your salvation - having also believed, you were sealed in Him with the Holy Spirit of promise, who is given as a pledge of our inheritance, with a view to the redemption of God's own possession, to the praise of His glory."

2) Train for Godliness. The Holy Spirit authenticates you (verifies who you are!) as one who belongs to Jesus Christ. You are a member of God's team, and the victory is secured through the seal of the Holy Spirit; therefore, live like a champion today!

"For as many as are the promises of God, in Him they are yes; therefore also through Him is our Amen to the glory of God through us. Now He who establishes us with you in Christ and anointed us is God, who also sealed us and gave us the Spirit in our hearts as a pledge" (2 Corinthians 1:20-22).

Think of all the software that's out there that does facial or thumbprint recognition. In the context of that image, it's as if, when our identity is checked, the Holy Spirit's presence in us allows us to be identified as Christ-like, and not merely as ourselves. We have the thumbprint of Christ in us because we have the Holy Spirit. Holiness is the Holy Spirit in you – God abiding in you – not that you are doing certain things, but that holy activities are flowing from God's holy presence in you!

3) Listen to the Coach. The sealing happens when you receive Jesus Christ as your Lord and Savior. If you have not yet received Jesus Christ as your Lord and Savior, then you are still dead in your sins, and your spirit has not yet been quickened to life through the indwelling of God's Holy Spirit.

"However, you are not in the flesh but in the Spirit, if indeed the Spirit of God dwells in you. But if anyone does not have the Spirit of

Christ, he does not belong to Him. If Christ is in you, though the body is dead because of sin, yet the spirit is alive because of righteousness. But if the Spirit of Him who raised Jesus from the dead dwells in you, He who raised Christ Jesus from the dead will also give life to your mortal bodies through His Spirit who dwells in you" (Romans 8:9-11).

The gifts of the Spirit demonstrate our ministry and the fruit of the Spirit authenticates that we are in Christ Jesus. Not a single person can live the Christian life apart from the seal of the Holy Spirit. He authenticates us as belonging to Christ – members of God's team!

4) Work together with God's team. The Holy Spirit is the "pledge of our inheritance," meaning that the Holy Spirit guarantees delivery to the intended destination of Heaven.

"Do not grieve the Holy Spirit of God, by whom you were sealed for the day of redemption" (Ephesians 4:30).

When you think of the Holy Spirit, you can think of the mail, or a carrier service you trust. We seal, address, and stamp a letter for the USPS expecting it to get to the address it was intended. A seal is a sign of both ownership and authorship! We are sent by God to do His will; we are under His authority!

"There is one body and one Spirit, just as also you were called in one hope of your calling" (Ephesians 4:4).

The Holy Spirit is the sign – the seal – of the authority and power by which we are authorized, and through which we are empowered, to accomplish God's will. We are bound together with God, and with one another, as the body of Christ through the seal of the Holy Spirit. Therefore, run the race faithfully today and execute the play of the day for the glory of God.

Day 12 Promise 12
The Promise of Unity

1) Know God's Playbook: The play of the day is John 17:11:

"I am no longer in the world; and yet they themselves are in the world, and I come to You. Holy Father, keep them in Your name, the name which You have given Me, that they may be one even as We are."

2) Train for Godliness. Athletes must learn to keep the first thing first in their training regimen. It is easy to be distracted by numbers in the weight room, or calories in the diet, but the purpose for training must always remain first – winning the victory! For Christian athletes, the victory is the glory of God through His Son Jesus Christ.

"He is also head of the body, the church; and He is the beginning, the firstborn from the dead, so that He Himself will come to have first place in everything" (Colossians 1:18).

Keeping Jesus preeminent in our lives brings about unity in three ways:

1. **Christian unity is in Christ alone!** When we are disunified, it means we have lost focus on Him and made it about us!
2. **Christian unity is on mission for God!** When we are disunified, it means we are off God's mission and into our own agendas – social, political, religious, or personal!
3. **Christian unity is for God's glory alone!** When we want the attention or credit for the good works done, then God is not glorified!

3) Listen to the Coach. According to Jesus' prayer, the unity of God's people is intended to reflect the very unity of God Himself, as He has revealed Himself to us as Father, Son, and Holy Spirit!

"I do not ask on behalf of these alone, but for those also who believe in Me through their word; that they may all be one; even as You,

Father, are in Me and I in You, that they also may be in Us, so that the world may believe that You sent Me. The glory which You have given Me I have given to them, that they may be one, just as We are one; I in them and You in Me, that they may be perfected in unity, so that the world may know that You sent Me, and loved them, even as You have loved Me" (John 17:20-23).

This is our greatest gift, and our hardest fruit – our unity which bears the very nature of the Godhead. With this rich understanding that our unity needs to rise above all human boundaries and distinctions, as well as all human fear and ambition, let us pray in agreement with Jesus' prayer for God's team. Prayer changes things because prayer changes us!

4) Work together with God's team. Expressing our unity with God, and one another, is our mission in today's divided world. Paul's call to unity in the Church is anchored in Christ's work to adopt us into the one family of God – heirs to the promises of God.

"For you are all sons of God through faith in Christ Jesus. For all of you who were baptized into Christ have clothed yourselves with Christ. There is neither Jew nor Greek, there is neither slave nor free man, there is neither male nor female; for you are all one in Christ Jesus. And if you belong to Christ, then you are Abraham's descendants, heirs according to promise" (Galatians 3:26-29).

Your union with Christ is made manifest by your unity within the body of Christ. Just like it is obvious when a sports team is unified in purpose and has trained itself to accomplish that purpose together, so it is obvious when the Church of Jesus Christ is focused on "His kingdom and His righteousness" (Matthew 6:33). The promise of unity in the Church is how the world will see Jesus Christ exalted and lifted high! Therefore, run the race faithfully today and execute the play of the day for the glory of God.

Day 13 Promise 13
The Promise of Peace with God

1) Know God's Playbook. The play of the day is John 14:27:

"Peace I leave with you; My peace I give to you; not as the world gives do I give to you. Do not let your heart be troubled, nor let it be fearful."

2) Train for Godliness. Peace with God is your salvation. It manifests as your holiness, which is God in you through the indwelling of the Holy Spirit. Jesus defeated the power of death, and the forces of evil, to restore us back into right relationship with the Father. Christ has made the way!

"For it was the Father's good pleasure for all the fullness to dwell in Him, and through Him to reconcile all things to Himself, having made peace through the blood of His cross; through Him, I say, whether things on earth or things in heaven" (Colossians 1:19-20).

"Therefore, having been justified by faith, we have peace with God through our Lord Jesus Christ, through whom also we have obtained our introduction by faith into this grace in which we stand; and we exult in hope of the glory of God" (Romans 5:1-2).

3) Listen to the Coach. Peace with God doesn't change the reality that we live in a broken world. While the promise of peace is paired with Jesus' promise that we will have tribulations, it also assures us that we no longer have to face them alone – God is with us!

"These things I have spoken to you, so that in Me you may have peace. In the world you have tribulation but take courage; I have overcome the world" (John 16:33).

The victorious life is the daily life of trusting God that His commands for our lives are for our good and His glory! You can trust His playbook and be confident the Coach knows what He is doing! We live like a champion when we trust that following His ways will bring about the desired purpose. When we submit to His Word, we have peace with God – we are being faithful, and He will do the rest. Peace with God puts the burden for results and outcomes squarely on God's shoulders, and frees us to live with joy and peace.

"So will My word be which goes forth from My mouth; it will not return to Me empty, without accomplishing what I desire, and without succeeding in the matter for which I sent it. For you will go out with joy and be led forth with peace; the mountains and the hills will break forth into shouts of joy before you, and all the trees of the field will clap their hands" (Isaiah 55:11-12).

4) Work together with God's team. In partnerships like marriage, when both parties are focused on Christ and growing closer to Him, their lives converge and there is peace. But when each person is chasing after his or her own life or happiness, then their lives diverge and there is no lasting peace. Peace with God brings like-mindedness to the athletes of God so that they can run the right play at the right time according to the will of God for their lives.

"Beyond all these things put on love, which is the perfect bond of unity. Let the peace of Christ rule in your hearts, to which indeed you were called in one body; and be thankful. Let the word of Christ richly dwell within you, with all wisdom teaching and admonishing one another with psalms and hymns and spiritual songs, singing with thankfulness in your hearts to God. Whatever you do in word or deed, do all in the name of the Lord Jesus, giving thanks through Him to God the Father" (Colossians 3:14-17).

Peace with God is what leads to a life of wholeness with yourself, and health with others. Therefore, run the race faithfully today and execute the play of the day for the glory of God.

Day 14 Promise 14
The Promise of a Teacher

1) Know God's Playbook. The play of the day is Luke 12:11-12:

"When they bring you before the synagogues and the rulers and the authorities, do not worry about how or what you are to speak in your defense, or what you are to say; for the Holy Spirit will teach you in that very hour what you ought to say."

2) Train for Godliness. Jesus Christ's call to follow Him and become His disciple is a call to be His apprentice – a student to the Master Teacher.

"Take My yoke upon you and learn from Me" (Matthew 11:29a).

Every coach knows that young athletes need more experienced training partners who can encourage them in their training regimen, teach them proper technique, help them with the playbook, and give the more novice athlete a goal to work towards. Very often, the coach intends for the athlete to aspire to become like, or to exceed, the assigned mentors.

"A pupil is not above his teacher; but everyone, after he has been fully trained, will be like his teacher" (Luke 6:40).

Jesus is our standard in every area of life, not just in our faith and practice. He set an example for us that we are to follow, taught us all that we need to know, and promised us the Holy Spirit to be our Teacher, who will assist us in our training for Godliness.

"These things I have spoken to you while abiding with you. But the Helper, the Holy Spirit, whom the Father will send in My name, He will teach you all things, and bring to your remembrance all that I said to you" (John 14:25-26; cf. 15:26-27).

3) Listen to the Coach. It is every athlete's responsibility to learn the voice of his or her coach, and to listen attentively when the coach speaks. When I was competing, no matter the size of venue, I could hear my coach's voice and would pay attention to what he was saying. His voice received priority over all other voices! With God as our Coach, we must learn to know and trust His voice above all others; that only happens by spending time with Him, the Good Shepherd of our soul!

"When he puts forth all his own, he goes ahead of them, and the sheep follow him because they know his voice" (John 10:4).

"But when He, the Spirit of truth, comes, He will guide you into all the truth; for He will not speak on His own initiative, but whatever He hears, He will speak; and He will disclose to you what is to come. He will glorify Me, for He will take of Mine and will disclose it to you. All things that the Father has are Mine; therefore I said that He takes of Mine and will disclose it to you" (John 16:13-15).

4) Work together with God's team. Our efforts are coordinated when we all learn to listen to the Holy Spirit. We do this by reading God's Word and praying according to His promises. You are to learn the distinctiveness of the Coach's voice, and the character of His playbook, so that you are ready to run the right play at the right time, in a coordinated effort with the other members of God's team.

"This book of the law shall not depart from your mouth, but you shall meditate on it day and night, so that you may be careful to do according to all that is written in it; for then you will make your way prosperous, and then you will have success" (Joshua 1:8).

When the team huddles, each athlete must be ready to listen, then do his or her part to run the play. This promise prepares you to be successful in all your ways. Therefore, run the race faithfully today and execute the play of the day for the glory of God.

Day 15 Promise 15
The Promise of Calling

1) Know God's Playbook. The play of the day is Ephesians 4:1:

"Therefore I, the prisoner of the Lord, implore you to walk in a manner worthy of the calling with which you have been called."

2) Train for Godliness. Every athlete of God has a calling. This sounds simple, but it addresses a huge misunderstanding in the traditional church that must be addressed if you are going to live like a champion today – the calling of God is not limited to being a pastor or missionary. The calling of God is for every single believer in Jesus because the calling of God is about the health and functionality of the entire body of Christ.

"There is one body and one Spirit, just as also you were called in one hope of your calling; one Lord, one faith, one baptism, one God and Father of all who is over all and through all and in all"
(Ephesians 4:4-6).

God's will for each of our lives is that we reflect Him – that we walk in a manner worthy of that calling – to be "conformed to the image of His Son."

"For those whom He foreknew, He also predestined to become conformed to the image of His Son, so that He would be the firstborn among many brethren; and these whom He predestined, He also called; and these whom He called, He also justified; and these whom He justified, He also glorified" (Romans 8:29-30).

This is your first calling, and every other call is secondary to it! Your first calling is God's preeminent purpose for your life: to walk with Him in a manner worthy of His calling – to walk like Jesus walked!

"By this we know that we are in Him: the one who says he abides in Him ought himself to walk in the same manner as He walked"
(1 John 2:5b-6).

3) Listen to the Coach. The daily training regimen of God's athletes is to learn how Jesus walked and follow Him, by the power of the Spirit and for the glory of God! This is our victory – to grow up (mature) into Christlikeness!

"Speaking the truth in love, we are to grow up in all aspects into Him who is the head, even Christ, from whom the whole body, being fitted and held together by what every joint supplies, according to the proper working of each individual part, causes the growth of the body for the building up of itself in love" (Ephesians 4:15-16).

You are called to be a part of something bigger than you! Are you "all in?" Are you committed and submitted to a local congregation? This is where God calls you to work out your salvation, in real time with real people, to mature with one another through the Spirit's work in the body.

4) Work together with God's team. You have been chosen by God and called to be a member of the body of Christ so that we, as one mature body, walk in a manner worthy of our calling! What would a team look like if each member was to start running his or her own play? It would be chaos! The coach unifies the team by calling the play. When each athlete submits to that plan, the members of the team can focus their efforts for a greater good. In Christ, we are better together than we are alone!

"For just as we have many members in one body and all the members do not have the same function, so we, who are many, are one body in Christ, and individually members one of another" (Romans 12:4-5).

Pursuing Christlikeness is a team sport that requires each of us to train ourselves according to the promise and then be a healthy, cooperative, functional member of God's family. The victory belongs to Jesus, and He has given it to us to make visible for all to see – this is our calling! Therefore, run the race faithfully today and execute the play of the day for the glory of God.

Day 16 Promise 16
The Promise of Forgiveness

1) Know God's Playbook: The play of the day is 1 John 1:9:

"If we confess our sins, He is faithful and righteous to forgive us our sins and to cleanse us from all unrighteousness."

2) Train for Godliness: Forgiveness is a foundational promise to the victorious life. When I was training for the Olympics, I was encouraged by the testimony of a professional athlete – an accomplished champion – who would go back to his high school coach every off season to focus on the basics of his sport. We must do the same as Christians!

Dr. Art Patzia, one of my seminary professors at Fuller taught me in a moment of personal crisis, "Christianity comes down to this one word - forgiveness!" In that moment, I learned this to be profoundly true! I had already confessed my sin to God and knew I was forgiven, but after I confessed my sin to the person I had sinned against, I experienced freedom from that sin and a fresh outpouring of God's empowerment for my daily living. This can be a reality that keeps our conscience clean and our connection with God open.

"Therefore, confess your sins to one another, and pray for one another so that you may be healed. The effective prayer of a righteous man can accomplish much" (James 5:16).

Unconfessed sin is like having a tight muscle, which, if left unattended, can become an injury that makes you ineffective and can even take you off the playing field for a season. In the same way that stretching is an essential and effective part of an athlete's daily regimen to both protect and prepare his or her body for greater feats of athletic prowess, so confessing our sins to God, and to one another, is the means of grace by which we protect and prepare our hearts, minds, and souls for greater effectiveness as God's athletes.

3) Listen to the Coach: Jesus was clear when He taught His disciples how to pray. Communication with God includes the asking for forgiveness of sin and the giving of forgiveness to those who have sinned against us. As an athlete of God, you are invited to join with Jesus and pray the Lord's Prayer in the morning and evening (Matthew 6:9-13).

"And forgive us our debts, as we also have forgiven our debtors" (Matthew 6:12).

"For if you forgive others for their transgressions, your heavenly Father will also forgive you. But if you do not forgive others, then your Father will not forgive your transgressions" (Matthew 6:14-15; cf. 2 Corinthians 2:10-11).

4) Work together with God's team: If God's team – the Church – should be known for one thing, it is forgiveness! This is the most fundamental play in God's playbook and, as His athletes, the Coach is calling upon us to pray it, train it, and practice it as a team. This is our identity in Christ – "Let the redeemed of the Lord say so" (Psalm 107:2)!

"Therefore if you are presenting your offering at the altar, and there remember that your brother has something against you, leave your offering there before the altar and go; first be reconciled to your brother, and then come and present your offering" (Matthew 5:23-24; cf. Matthew 18:21-35).

This is how the world knows who we are – our love for one another through the giving and receiving of forgiveness (John 13:34-35). May we faithfully run the play of forgiveness, so the world may know that, regardless of what the scoreboard says at halftime, God wins and His team members are the champions! Therefore, run the race faithfully today and execute the play of the day for the glory of God.

Day 17 Promise 17
The Promise of the Peace of God

1) Know God's Playbook. The play of the day is Philippians 4:6-7:

"Be anxious for nothing, but in everything by prayer and supplication with thanksgiving let your requests be made known to God. And the peace of God, which surpasses all comprehension, will guard your hearts and your minds in Christ Jesus."

2) Train for Godliness. The peace of God that surpasses all comprehension is not the peace the world has to offer; it is the peace of God that has been given to us through the Holy Spirit (John 14:27). It is a fruit of the Spirit (Galatians 5:22-23). This peace is to rule over our hearts and lead our lives (Colossians 3:14-17). This is our salvation alive in us – Christ in us!

Paul practically teaches us about how to walk in His peace. It is one thing to say you are saved, and another to experience spiritual vitality through His peace protecting your mind and heart in Christ Jesus – your wholeness in Him! The imagery Paul used is of God, like a military guard, standing at the doorpost of your heart and mind and not letting any unhealthy or unwholesome thing come in. God is protecting you from the devil, who wants to use tribulations to get a foothold in your life.

"For though we walk in the flesh, we do not war according to the flesh, for the weapons of our warfare are not of the flesh, but divinely powerful for the destruction of fortresses. We are destroying speculations and every lofty thing raised up against the knowledge of God, and we are taking every thought captive to the obedience of Christ" (2 Corinthians 10:3-5).

"Be angry, and yet do not sin; do not let the sun go down on your anger, and do not give the devil an opportunity" (Ephesians 4:26-27).

Paul wants us to experience victory in every human emotion throughout life's journey. Through the Holy Spirit, God is helping you learn how to win the victory by capturing your thoughts, that you may live the life of prayer and thanksgiving to God. God has given you everything you need to live like a champion today!

3) Listen to the Coach. God loves you and cares about you; this is the truth that gives you the confidence to approach the throne of grace and cast all your anxiety upon Him.

> **"Therefore humble yourselves under the mighty hand of God, that He may exalt you at the proper time, casting all your anxiety on Him, because He cares for you" (1 Peter 5:6-7).**

> **"Therefore let us draw near with confidence to the throne of grace, so that we may receive mercy and find grace to help in time of need" (Hebrews 4:16).**

4) Work together with God's team. The peace of God manifests as your holiness as you learn to love God with all your heart, and with all your soul, and with all your mind! This promise of peace not only restores you back into right relationship with God, but, because of the love of God, you can now have peace with yourself first, then with others. It is through this peace that we, as members of the Body of Christ, can ultimately satisfy the Greatest Commandments.

> **"'You shall love the Lord your God with all your heart, and with all your soul, and with all your mind.' This is the great and foremost commandment. The second is like it, 'You shall love your neighbor as yourself.' On these two commandments depend the whole Law and the Prophets" (Matthew 22:37-40).**

This requires God's peace to come from above, into you, and then through you to others. You are a conduit of God's love because His peace is designed to transform you into a peacemaker, or minister of reconciliation. This is the victory of God in us and through us! Therefore, run the race faithfully today and execute the play of the day for the glory of God.

Day 18 Promise 18
The Promise of Rest

1) Know God's Playbook. The play of the day is Matthew 11:28-30:

"Come to Me, all who are weary and heavy-laden, and I will give you rest. Take My yoke upon you and learn from Me, for I am gentle and humble in heart, and you will find rest for your souls. For My yoke is easy and My burden is light."

2) Train for Godliness. Most champions have a driven, goal-oriented personality; they desire to give themselves wholeheartedly to a goal. Their issue is not one of failing to train hard enough; often, their failure is overtraining. When you don't give your body the rest intervals it needs to recover, it leads to injuries, chronic fatigue, depression, and nervous breakdowns. A teammate of mine committed suicide after not making the Olympic team. It was devastating! He was most likely overtrained and had lost perspective under the heavy weight of his grief.

When Jesus made His gracious offer of rest, to "all who are weary and heavy-burdened" (28), He was offering them a personal relationship with God (through the yoke imagery). He would teach them to live in alignment with God's rescue from slavery to sin, the sin that seeks to weigh us down and crush our spirits.

"Let us also lay aside every encumbrance and the sin which so easily entangles us, and let us run with endurance the race that is set before us, fixing our eyes on Jesus, the author and perfecter of faith, ... so that you will not grow weary and lose heart" (Hebrews 12:1-3).

Jesus' promise is the life of faith in God – trusting the Father's sovereign plan, the Son's sufficient provision, and the Spirit's sustaining power. This is why we are to take on Jesus' easy yoke of faith in His Father!

"It was for freedom that Christ set us free; therefore keep standing firm and do not be subject again to a yoke of slavery" (Galatians 5:1).

3) Listen to the Coach. The world teaches you to rest *after* you work, but God invites you to learn how to work *from* the place of rest. The yoke of

Jesus Christ is "easy," which means it is custom-made – well-fitted for you personally. Jesus invites each athlete to grow in a personal relationship with Him, so that He can pace and direct his or her life. The Coach's call to a life of devotion includes a right rhythm of rest and work.

"So there remains a Sabbath rest for the people of God. For the one who has entered His rest has himself also rested from his works, as God did from His. Therefore let us be diligent to enter that rest, so that no one will fall, through following the same example of disobedience" (Hebrews 4:9-11).

Taking time to rest with God includes prioritizing gathering with your church family, eating a meal with others, taking a nap, having fun, trusting God's provision for your life by ceasing from the work that dominates your other six days, and taking time to delight in God's rich bounty of food and drink. You were designed to enjoy God for an eternity – start today!

4) Work together with God's team. Jesus restored the sabbath to its original intent so that God's team can experience rest as a part of the sacred rhythm of human life (Genesis 2:1-3). Your rest in God's loving gift of sabbath is just as important as the work you do on the playing field of life (the Harvest!).

"For the Son of Man is Lord of the Sabbath" (Matthew 12:8).

An essential practice of finishing strong in the Christian life is staying in rhythm with Jesus Christ, in His easy yoke. Jesus is both the Lord of the Sabbath and the Lord of the Harvest. All work and no rest hinders God's athletes from living like a champion today. You can't afford *not* to rest! Therefore, run the race faithfully today and execute the play of the day for the glory of God.

Day 19 Promise 19
The Promise of an Anointing

1) Know God's Playbook. The play of the day is 1 John 2:20:

"But you have an anointing from the Holy One, and you all know."

2) Train for Godliness. It is the anointing of the Holy Spirit that fulfills, in and through us, the promises of God. This was true for Jesus, whose ministry was fulfilled through the anointing of God upon Him.

"And the book of the prophet Isaiah was handed to Him. And He opened the book and found the place where it was written, 'The Spirit of the Lord is upon Me, because He anointed Me to preach the gospel to the poor. He has sent Me to proclaim release to the captives, and recovery of sight to the blind, to set free those who are oppressed, to proclaim the favorable year of the Lord.' And He closed the book, gave it back to the attendant and sat down; and the eyes of all in the synagogue were fixed on Him. And He began to say to them, 'Today this Scripture has been fulfilled in your hearing'" (Luke 4:18-21).

The anointing of the Holy Spirit is not about gaining a special status or position in the church through secret knowledge, or increased revelation; the anointing is what makes each of us a Christian in the first place. When a person is anointed, or when we say there was an anointing on a service or worship time or sermon, what we are saying is that the presence and power of the Holy Spirit was manifested, or evidenced, by people's encounters with Him. To walk in the anointing is God's desire for every believer – so you can live like a champion today.

"As for you, the anointing which you received from Him abides in you, and you have no need for anyone to teach you; but as His anointing teaches you about all things, and is true and is not a lie, and just as it has taught you, you abide in Him" (1 John 2:27).

3) Listen to the Coach. The anointing is God's way of setting apart His people for His glory. Walking in the anointing begins with believing God for who He says you are as a member of His team and living your life for the victory He has bestowed upon you. Listening to God requires you to believe that what He says about you being a member of His team is true.

> **"But you are a chosen race, a royal priesthood, a holy nation, a people for God's own possession, so that you may proclaim the excellencies of Him who has called you out of darkness into His marvelous light; for you once were not a people, but now you are the people of God; you had not received mercy, but now you have received mercy. Beloved, I urge you as aliens and strangers to abstain from fleshly lusts which wage war against the soul. Keep your behavior excellent among the Gentiles, so that in the thing in which they slander you as evildoers, they may because of your good deeds, as they observe them, glorify God in the day of visitation" (1 Peter 2:9-12).**

4) Work together with God's team. As much as it is impossible for you to be a member of God's team without God's anointing, it is impossible for you *not* to be a member of His team *with* the anointing. You are His anointed!

> **"I will ask the Father, and He will give you another Helper, that He may be with you forever; that is the Spirit of truth, whom the world cannot receive, because it does not see Him or know Him, but you know Him because He abides with you and will be in you. I will not leave you as orphans; I will come to you" (John 14:16-18).**

You and your teammates have everything needed to be secure and successful to win the victory. Therefore, run the race faithfully today and execute the play of the day for the glory of God.

Day 20 Promise 20
The Promise of the Ministry of Reconciliation

1) Know God's Playbook. The play of the day is 2 Corinthians 5:18-19:

"Now all these things are from God, who reconciled us to Himself through Christ and gave us the ministry of reconciliation, namely, that God was in Christ reconciling the world to Himself, not counting their trespasses against them, and He has committed to us the word of reconciliation."

2) Train for Godliness. The peace with God that guards our hearts and minds in Christ Jesus is our greatest witness, as it brings external peace between us and other people. We are actively taking the gift God gave us and giving it to others – right relationship!

"But now in Christ Jesus you who formerly were far off have been brought near by the blood of Christ. For He Himself is our peace, who made both groups into one and broke down the barrier of the dividing wall, by abolishing in His flesh the enmity, which is the Law of commandments contained in ordinances, so that in Himself He might make the two into one new man, thus establishing peace, and might reconcile them both in one body to God through the cross, by it having put to death the enmity" (Ephesians 2:13-16).

Passing the peace is more than a handshake on Sunday mornings, it is the Church's mission! It's hard work! Through the presence of the Holy Spirit, you are to build bridges with people to unite them in Christ alone – Jesus is our peace! This is the gospel work of the Church because we are called ministers of reconciliation, or, as Jesus called us, peacemakers.

"Blessed are the peacemakers, for they shall be called sons of God"
(Matthew 5:9).

3) Listen to the Coach. Jesus teaches that the ministry of reconciliation is paramount and practical. It is a good idea, and the right thing to do – it is the right play at the right time, every time! Every single one of our meetings is about this before it is about budgets, buildings, or programs.

"Therefore if you are presenting your offering at the altar, and there remember that your brother has something against you, leave your offering there before the altar and go; first be reconciled to your brother, and then come and present your offering" (Matthew 5:23-24).

Reconciliation is the hardest work of the Church! Jesus commanded it in Matthew 5:25, and Paul rebuked us for not doing it in 1 Corinthians 6:1-11. We are the people of God, reconciled unto the Father through the Son, called to run the play of reconciliation in such a way as to build the team and not tear it down.

"Brethren, even if anyone is caught in any trespass, you who are spiritual, restore such a one in a spirit of gentleness; each one looking to yourself, so that you too will not be tempted. Bear one another's burdens, and thereby fulfill the law of Christ" (Galatians 6:1-2).

4) Work together with God's team. The ministry of reconciliation is a team sport that requires everyone to do their part. We are in this together!

"But God demonstrates His own love toward us, in that while we were yet sinners, Christ died for us" (Romans 5:8).

"You are the light of the world. A city set on a hill cannot be hidden; nor does anyone light a lamp and put it under a basket, but on the lampstand, and it gives light to all who are in the house. Let your light shine before men in such a way that they may see your good works, and glorify your Father who is in heaven" (Matthew 5:14-16).

The "us" in Romans 5:8 is critical to our ability to pass the peace. It's not a "me" thing; we are in this together as God's team. We are the people of God, not I alone, but us together. We are the "city set on a hill" that is to shine brightly for the world to see and not be hidden. Therefore, run the race faithfully today and execute the play of the day for the glory of God.

Day 21 Promise 21
The Promise of the God of Peace

1) Know God's Playbook. The play of the day is Philippians 4:8-9:

"Finally, brethren, whatever is true, whatever is honorable, whatever is right, whatever is pure, whatever is lovely, whatever is of good repute, if there is any excellence and if anything worthy of praise, dwell on these things. The things you have learned and received and heard and seen in me, practice these things, and the God of peace will be with you."

2) Train for Godliness. God's athletes are to remain faithful in the habits of grace that will wash over their hearts and minds, so that they are not taken hostage by any situation. Each crisis comes with its own challenges, but all are opportunities to grow in God's grace and mercy – to be closer to Him. In Him, we can experience rest and peace, even when these temporary dwelling places (our bodies, which include our brains) are experiencing the brokenness of the fall. These bodies need healing and only One can do that – the God of peace!

In the same way that you must remain positive and hopeful in your treatment plans for other medical issues, you are invited to remain vigilant to capture your thoughts in times of crisis (2 Corinthians 10:5). This includes shattering the old broken tapes, stopping the stinking thinking, and ceasing the catastrophic ideation, in order to give yourself the best chance possible of experiencing the God of peace abiding in you. He commands you to think right thoughts and do right deeds; He will respond with His presence.

"This book of the law shall not depart from your mouth, but you shall meditate on it day and night, so that you may be careful to do according to all that is written in it; for then you will make your way prosperous, and then you will have success. Have I not commanded you? Be strong and courageous! Do not tremble or be dismayed, for the LORD your God is with you wherever you go" (Joshua 1:8-9).

3) Listen to the Coach. "And the God of peace will be with you." Peace is the very essence of God; He is Jehovah Shalom (Judges 6:34-34). Peace is God with you – His wholeness in a situation! That is what shalom means, and this is God's desire for His covenanted people (Isaiah 26:3-4, 12; 54:10; 66:12-13) – peace with Him!

Victory comes from God's presence with you, by which you learn to live in God's grace. God's grace is not just your heavenly position before God (your salvation), it is the power source by which you live and have your being on Earth (Acts 17:24-28). God's grace is your sufficiency for all things because it is the God of peace at work in you!

> **"And [Jesus] has said to me, 'My grace is sufficient for you, for power is perfected in weakness.' Most gladly, therefore, I will rather boast about my weaknesses, so that the power of Christ may dwell in me. Therefore I am well content with weaknesses, with insults, with distresses, with persecutions, with difficulties, for Christ's sake; for when I am weak, then I am strong" (2 Corinthians 12:9-10).**

4) Work together with God's team. We are to love our teammates as we love ourselves – by the grace of God and through the peace that He has bestowed upon us through His Son Jesus Christ.

> **"Finally, brethren, rejoice, be made complete, be comforted, be like-minded, live in peace; and the God of love and peace will be with you. Greet one another with a holy kiss. All the saints greet you. The grace of the Lord Jesus Christ, and the love of God, and the fellowship of the Holy Spirit, be with you all" (2 Corinthians 13:11-14).**

When you live in the fellowship of the Father, Son, and Holy Spirit, you are transformed into His likeness and are made complete by the presence of Jehovah Shalom abiding in you. It's teamwork – the work of the Godhead in you and in every member of His team! Therefore, run the race faithfully today and execute the play of the day for the glory of God.

Day 22 Promise 22
The Promise of Intercession

1) Know God's Playbook. The play of the day is Romans 8:34:

"Christ Jesus is He who died, yes, rather who was raised, who is at the right hand of God, who also intercedes for us."

2) Train for Godliness. The promise of Jesus' intercession is the fulfillment of His ascension (Acts 1:1-11). Because of Jesus' ascension, even if you don't know how, or what, to pray, you can relax because Jesus is already praying for you. Simultaneously, the Holy Spirit, who dwells in you, and Jesus, who is at the right of the Father in Heaven, are speaking with one another, and with the Father, about you. That is life-altering good news – mysterious and miraculous! You have an Advocate who has won the victory for you and will never stop fighting for you to experience His victory!

"In the same way the Spirit also helps our weakness; for we do not know how to pray as we should, but the Spirit Himself intercedes for us with groanings too deep for words; and He who searches the hearts knows what the mind of the Spirit is, because He intercedes for the saints according to the will of God. And we know that God causes all things to work together for good to those who love God, to those who are called according to His purpose" (Romans 8:26-28).

Your hope is not simply for this life, but for eternal life (1 Corinthians 15:19); Jesus' resurrection and ascension are essential to our hope, and critical to our understanding of this body and its future along with all creation, in the New Heaven and New Earth (Revelation 21-22). You are a promised participant in His ascension (Ephesians 2:4-7). The ascension of Jesus Christ invites you to live faithfully and to keep your focus on Jesus and His Kingdom.

"Therefore if you have been raised up with Christ, keep seeking the things above, where Christ is, seated at the right hand of God. Set your mind on the things above, not on the things that are on earth" (Colossians 3:1-2).

3) Listen to the Coach. The Coach wants to hear from you, personally, because Jesus is already talking to Him about you. Jesus, being at the right hand of the Father, has the authority of Heaven for both earthly and heavenly affairs, which includes every detail of your life. He invites you to come into agreement with His will – His purposes are good!

"[Jesus] is at the right hand of God, having gone into heaven, after angels and authorities and powers had been subjected to Him" (1 Peter 3:22; cf. Ephesians 1:18-23; Philippians 2:9-11).

You are invited to respond to the fears and anxieties of this life by declaring the victory of Jesus Christ, through thanksgiving and through prayers and supplications. Then you may experience God's powerful presence over all things that seek to deter you from being faithful to the Coach. He has empowered you through His intercession to execute the right play at the right time.

"Be anxious for nothing, but in everything by prayer and supplication with thanksgiving let your requests be made known to God. And the peace of God, which surpasses all comprehension, will guard your hearts and your minds in Christ Jesus" (Philippians 4:6-7).

4) Work together with God's team. God's intervention is through Jesus' intercession and that is only possible because of the ascension (Hebrews 1:1-4)!

"This Jesus God raised up again, to which we are all witnesses. Therefore having been exalted to the right hand of God, and having received from the Father the promise of the Holy Spirit, He has poured forth this which you both see and hear" (Acts 2:32-33).

God is with you through His presence and power living in you! May God be exalted in and through His team, beginning with you living like a champion today! Therefore, run the race faithfully today and execute the play of the day for the glory of God.

Day 23 Promise 23
The Promise of Transformation

1) Know God's Playbook. The play of the day is Romans 12:2:

"Do not be conformed to this world, but be transformed by the renewing of your mind, so that you may prove what the will of God is, that which is good and acceptable and perfect."

2) Train for Godliness. You are invited to live as the new creation of God as the Holy Spirit transforms you through the renewal of your mind. This is God's will for your life as you respond to the mercy of God by presenting yourself holy to God and trust the Spirit of God at work in your life.

"Therefore I urge you, brethren, by the mercies of God, to present your bodies a living and holy sacrifice, acceptable to God, which is your spiritual service of worship" (Romans 12:1).

We participate in this process through our personal faith practices, called spiritual disciplines, and our community faith practices. It is in these unforced rhythms of grace that we are transformed by the renewing of our minds so that we represent Christ to the world as His Image Bearers.

3) Listen to the Coach. The Greek word translated "transformed" in Romans 12:2 is where we get the English word metamorphosis. This is the transformation – you become a new creature – from caterpillar to butterfly, from death to life! The promise of transformation only happens through partnership with the Holy Spirit, who actively works to renew your mind.

"Now we have received, not the spirit of the world, but the Spirit who is from God, so that we may know the things freely given to us by God, which things we also speak, not in words taught by human wisdom, but in those taught by the Spirit, combining spiritual thoughts with spiritual words. But a natural man does not accept the things of the Spirit of God, for they are foolishness to him; and he cannot understand them, because they are spiritually appraised. But he who is spiritual appraises all things, yet he himself is appraised by

no one. For who has known the mind of the Lord, that he will instruct Him? But we have the mind of Christ" (1 Corinthians 2:12-16).

To be transformed by the renewal of your mind is to have "the mind of Christ" and to appraise all things spiritually. The renewal of your mind prompts you not to conform to the patterns of this world, but to pray Heaven to Earth and work towards the answer to this prayer each day. "Thy will be done" is our prayer, as we join with Jesus in His prayer (Matthew 6:10)! This is how you prove God's will, "that which is good and acceptable and perfect," as promised in Romans 12:2.

4) Work together with God's team. With this transformational reality in mind, to "prove" is *not* an invitation to live your life in insecurity and fear, like a child on the playground saying to another, *"prove it!"* or like me saying to myself, *"I must prove to others (or to myself) that I am an athlete of God, that I really do deserve to be on God's team."* Proving, by this thought process, is opposed to grace and of the flesh.

"My Father is glorified by this, that you bear much fruit, and so prove to be My disciples" (John 15:8).

"Prove" in Romans 12:2 and John 15:8 means that God's work of transformation in you will demonstrate who you are by your new life of love through your union with Jesus Christ. Jesus invites you to bear fruit by abiding in the Vine (John 15:1-16), and to find rest for your soul by taking His easy yoke (Matthew 11:28-30). Paul invites you to give yourself to God as "a living and holy sacrifice" in response to His merciful gospel (Romans 12:1).

It is through your daily positive response to these invitations for union with Jesus Christ that God brings about your transformation through the renewal of your mind. Therefore, run the race faithfully today and execute the play of the day for the glory of God.

Day 24 Promise 24
The Promise of Good Works

1) Know God's Playbook. The play of the day is Ephesians 2:10:

"For we are His workmanship, created in Christ Jesus for good works, which God prepared beforehand so that we would walk in them."

2) Train for Godliness. God designed you on purpose! He shaped you and called you to use your life to glorify the Father through your good works. Learning what those good works are is often a journey of trying new things, serving in new ways, and even experiencing new jobs. We are invited to the long obedience of learning how to walk in the good works that God has prepared for us.

"Let us not lose heart in doing good, for in due time we will reap if we do not grow weary" (Galatians 6:9).

Furthermore, you must stay legit in your efforts to produce good works. I know what it is to be tempted to cheat or use performance enhancement drugs, but it is essential that our good works be submitted to, and in alignment with, God's calling. We work in partnership with the "God who is at work in [us], both to will and to work for His good pleasure" (Philippians 2:13).

"Now if any man builds on the foundation with gold, silver, precious stones, wood, hay, straw, each man's work will become evident; for the day will show it because it is to be revealed with fire, and the fire itself will test the quality of each man's work. If any man's work which he has built on it remains, he will receive a reward" (1 Corinthians 3:12-14).

3) Listen to the Coach. As an athlete, I would often go see a chiropractor to make sure my body was in alignment from head to toe. This is the very reason Jesus came and died on the Cross – for us to be aligned with the Father!

Jesus didn't die for workhorses, but for those who would "partake [partner] in His divine nature" (2 Peter 1:2-4). Jesus died so that we can be with the Father, aligned in relationship and in purpose (John 14:6).

"No longer do I call you slaves, for the slave does not know what his master is doing; but I have called you friends, for all things that I have heard from My Father I have made known to you. You did not choose Me but I chose you, and appointed you that you would go and bear fruit, and that your fruit would remain, so that whatever you ask of the Father in My name He may give to you" (John 15:15-16).

4) Work together with God's team. You were saved by grace alone, and the good news is that God's grace does not return void – grace always produces the results of God's intention (Isaiah 55:11)! You were saved by God's good work so that you would live out your life of good works for His glory!

"What use is it, my brethren, if someone says he has faith but he has no works? Can that faith save him? If a brother or sister is without clothing and in need of daily food, and one of you says to them, 'Go in peace, be warmed and be filled,' and yet you do not give them what is necessary for their body, what use is that? Even so faith, if it has no works, is dead, being by itself. But someone may well say, 'You have faith and I have works; show me your faith without the works, and I will show you my faith by my works'" (James 2:14-18).

The key to the promise of good works is not to focus on the work itself, but to focus on Jesus and learn what God has intended for you to uniquely do for Him. The good works that are done while abiding with Jesus are promised to follow you as a testimony of God's work in you (Revelation 14:12-13). Therefore, run the race faithfully today and execute the play of the day for the glory of God.

Day 25 Promise 25
The Promise of the Father's Discipline

1) Know God's Playbook. The play of the day is Hebrews 12:10-11:

"For they disciplined us for a short time as seemed best to them, but He disciplines us for our good, so that we may share His holiness. All discipline for the moment seems not to be joyful, but sorrowful; yet to those who have been trained by it, afterwards it yields the peaceful fruit of righteousness."

2) Train for Godliness. The Father's heart is for His children to have the character and attitude that accurately represent the family name. When you become a follower of Jesus, you are taking on the name of Christian (Acts 11:26), and it is God's desire for you to be conformed to the image of His Son (Romans 8:29). This is the purpose behind both the Father's discipline and His pruning – to ensure we manifest fruit in like kind to our namesake!

"I am the true vine, and My Father is the vinedresser. Every branch in Me that does not bear fruit, He takes away; and every branch that bears fruit, He prunes it so that it may bear more fruit. ... I am the vine, you are the branches; he who abides in Me and I in him, he bears much fruit, for apart from Me you can do nothing. If anyone does not abide in Me, he is thrown away as a branch and dries up; and they gather them, and cast them into the fire and they are burned" (John 15:1-2, 5-6).

"So every good tree bears good fruit, but the bad tree bears bad fruit. A good tree cannot produce bad fruit, nor can a bad tree produce good fruit. Every tree that does not bear good fruit is cut down and thrown into the fire. So then, you will know them by their fruits" (Matthew 7:17-20).

The fire in these passages does not represent damnation, but discipline! Every athlete knows what it is to be put through the fire – it is about refinement! The purpose of the Father's discipline is so that your life "yields the peaceful fruit of righteousness" (Hebrews 12:11).

3) Listen to the Coach. The Coach wants to see His reflection in you, which is why He puts all His athletes, including you, through the fire!

"In this you greatly rejoice, even though now for a little while, if necessary, you have been distressed by various trials, so that the proof of your faith, being more precious than gold which is perishable, even though tested by fire, may be found to result in praise and glory and honor at the revelation of Jesus Christ"
(1 Peter 1:6-7).

"Those whom I love, I reprove and discipline; therefore be zealous and repent. Behold, I stand at the door and knock; if anyone hears My voice and opens the door, I will come in to him and will dine with him, and he with Me. He who overcomes, I will grant to him to sit down with Me on My throne, as I also overcame and sat down with My Father on His throne" (Revelation 3:19-21).

4) Work together with God's team. When I was selected to represent Team USA, I no longer represented myself, or my school, or a sponsor; I represented my country. My character and attitude mattered to the coach, because we represented something so much bigger than ourselves. This truth is even more real when you are chosen as a member of God's team!

"It is for discipline that you endure; God deals with you as with sons; for what son is there whom his father does not discipline? But if you are without discipline, of which all have become partakers, then you are illegitimate children and not sons" (Hebrews 12:7-8).

You are a member of God's team, and it is only by coming under the discipline of the Coach's training regimen that the world will see and hear that you truly do belong to Him. Therefore, run the race faithfully today and execute the play of the day for the glory of God.

Day 26 Promise 26
The Promise of Freedom

1) Know God's Playbook. The play of the day is Galatians 5:1:

"It was for freedom that Christ set us free; therefore keep standing firm and do not be subject again to a yoke of slavery."

2) Train for Godliness. Believe God for His promises, rest in Jesus' easy yoke, and walk in the Holy Spirit. This is the faith that sets you free from sin to live for God. This is the covenant of grace that shatters the yoke of slavery, which Paul warns you not to take back upon yourself.

"So Jesus was saying to those Jews who had believed Him, 'If you continue in My word, then you are truly disciples of Mine; and you will know the truth, and the truth will make you free. … So if the Son makes you free, you will be free indeed'" (John 8:31-32, 36).

You must choose today which yoke you will put on and walk in – the yoke of slavery to sin, or the yoke of freedom in the Spirit! The hard yoke of the flesh is all about you taking matters into your own hands and striving to make life work out the way you think it should; the easy yoke of Jesus leads to freedom through trust in God for His plans and His ways to bring about what He promises.

"The thief comes only to steal and kill and destroy; I came that they may have life, and have it abundantly. I am the good shepherd; the good shepherd lays down His life for the sheep" (John 10:10-11).

3) Listen to the Coach. Listen to God and trust in His promises, and you will experience the fulfillment of the abundant life. Walk in the Spirit, who has given you everything you need for life and godliness (2 Peter 1:3). We are shaped by our life of devotion; therefore, put your hope in Jesus Christ and His victory and trust Him to fulfill your heart's desire in every area of your life (Matthew 6:33). Don't take matters into your own hands because, as soon you do, you will be gripped by whatever it is you're trying to control.

"Do you not know that when you present yourselves to someone as slaves for obedience, you are slaves of the one whom you obey, either of sin resulting in death, or of obedience resulting in righteousness? But thanks be to God that though you were slaves of sin, you became obedient from the heart to that form of teaching to which you were committed, and having been freed from sin, you became slaves of righteousness" (Romans 6:16-18).

Be careful to whom you listen and what promises you allow to get into your heart. Listen to the Coach, who has promised abundance, and not the thief, who only wants to deceive and destroy. There was a time in my athletic journey that I listened to some wrong voices; as those seeds took root in me, they corrupted my ambition, and I lost my joy and peace of my mind – my freedom (1 John 5:21)!

"For speaking out arrogant words of vanity they entice by fleshly desires, by sensuality, those who barely escape from the ones who live in error, promising them freedom while they themselves are slaves of corruption; for by what a man is overcome, by this he is enslaved" (2 Peter 2:18-19).

4) Work together with God's team. Stand firm together as God's team! Trust the Coach to call the right play at the right time!

"Only conduct yourselves in a manner worthy of the gospel of Christ, so that whether I come and see you or remain absent, I will hear of you that you are standing firm in one spirit, with one mind striving together for the faith of the gospel" (Philippians 1:27).

When we are united in our freedom in Christ, nothing can divide us or distract us from the victory we have been called to proclaim with our lives. Therefore, run the race faithfully today and execute the play of the day for the glory of God.

Day 27 Promise 27
The Promise of Power

1) Know God's Playbook. The play of the day is Acts 1:8:

"But you will receive power when the Holy Spirit has come upon you; and you shall be My witnesses both in Jerusalem, and in all Judea and Samaria, and even to the remotest part of the earth."

2) Train for Godliness. The key to the promise of power is the humility of the athlete to which it is entrusted – with power comes responsibility! Jesus modeled servant leadership for us throughout His ministry, but especially when He washed the feet of His disciples (John 13:5-17). Additionally, Jesus challenged His followers to use power differently than the world does; we are not to "lord it over" others, or "exercise authority" over them (Matthew 20:25-28).

"Therefore humble yourselves under the mighty hand of God, that He may exalt you at the proper time" (1 Peter 5:6).

As an athlete of God, you are invited to train your heart and mind according to the power of God through the Cross of Jesus Christ – this is our victory! This was Paul's power of ministry – the grace of God in and through Him to proclaim the gospel of Jesus Christ.

"For the word of the cross is foolishness to those who are perishing, but to us who are being saved it is the power of God. … For I determined to know nothing among you except Jesus Christ, and Him crucified. I was with you in weakness and in fear and in much trembling, and my message and my preaching were not in persuasive words of wisdom, but in demonstration of the Spirit and of power, so that your faith would not rest on the wisdom of men, but on the power of God" (1 Corinthians 1:18; 2:2-5).

3) Listen to the Coach. The power of the Holy Spirit equips our ability to know God's heart, and His direction for our lives, so that we can run the right play at the right time, and do so with confidence in His playbook. No matter the situation you are facing, God desires you, His athlete, to face it with His power, not your own!

"For God has not given us a spirit of timidity, but of power and love and discipline. Therefore do not be ashamed of the testimony of our Lord or of me His prisoner, but join with me in suffering for the gospel according to the power of God" (2 Timothy 1:7-8).

4) Work together with God's team. We are invited to join with Paul to exercise great power by praying for our teammates. May God's team walk in humility, wielding the power of God in prayer and love for the exaltation of Jesus Christ and His Kingdom come.

"We give thanks to God always for all of you, making mention of you in our prayers; constantly bearing in mind your work of faith and labor of love and steadfastness of hope in our Lord Jesus Christ in the presence of our God and Father, knowing, brethren beloved by God, His choice of you; for our gospel did not come to you in word only, but also in power and in the Holy Spirit and with full conviction; just as you know what kind of men we proved to be among you for your sake. You also became imitators of us and of the Lord, having received the word in much tribulation with the joy of the Holy Spirit, so that you became an example to all the believers in Macedonia and in Achaia" (1 Thessalonians 1:2-7).

"Now may the God of hope fill you with all joy and peace in believing, so that you will abound in hope by the power of the Holy Spirit" (Romans 15:13).

This is the work of the Holy Spirit – to bring about the promise of power in you to live like a champion today! Therefore, run the race faithfully today and execute the play of the day for the glory of God.

Day 28 Promise 28
The Promise of Greater Works

1) Know God's Playbook. The play of the day is John 14:12:

"Truly, truly, I say to you, he who believes in Me, the works that I do, he will do also; and greater works than these he will do; because I go to the Father."

2) Train for Godliness. The key to the promise of greater works is the life of believing God – trusting that the Coach will put you in at the right time to run the right play. It is not enough to believe in God, you must *believe* God for His promises! Timely application of God's Word must be trained into an athlete, so that the athlete can run the play under pressure.

"Therefore everyone who hears these words of Mine and acts on them, may be compared to a wise man who built his house on the rock. And the rain fell, and the floods came, and the winds blew and slammed against that house; and yet it did not fall, for it had been founded on the rock" (Matthew 7:24-25).

This promise is a call to trust God and His ways (Isaiah 55:8-13); therefore, keep as your greatest ambition, not the greater works themselves, but your walk of *believing* God. John the Elder stated in 3 John 4, "I have no greater joy than this, to hear of my children walking in the truth." Don't bail before the blessings – something bigger than you know is happening in your circumstances!

"The things that are impossible with people are possible with God" (Luke 18:27).

3) Listen to the Coach. The Coach has a different perspective on the game than the players on the field. He sees the victory when we can't! He seeks to work all things together, so He puts in the right athlete at the right time to run the right play. Each athlete must be ready to execute the play with a whole heart because the athlete trusts the Coach and His playbook. The job of the athlete is to trust the Coach!

"The men of Nineveh will stand up with this generation at the judgment, and will condemn it because they repented at the preaching of Jonah; and behold, something greater than Jonah is here. The Queen of the South will rise up with this generation at the judgment and will condemn it, because she came from the ends of the earth to hear the wisdom of Solomon; and behold, something greater than Solomon is here" (Matthew 12:41-42).

4) Work together with God's team. To accomplish the mission of God and see all nations blessed through the gospel of Jesus Christ, we are called to work together for the glory of God. To accomplish these bigger works, God gives us His power and presence so that we may be His authorized workers in the harvest fields.

"You will receive power when the Holy Spirit has come upon you; and you shall be My witnesses both in Jerusalem, and in all Judea and Samaria, and even to the remotest part of the earth" (Acts 1:8).

"All authority has been given to Me in heaven and on earth. Go therefore and make disciples of all the nations, baptizing them in the name of the Father and the Son and the Holy Spirit, teaching them to observe all that I commanded you; and lo, I am with you always, even to the end of the age" (Matthew 28:18-20).

You are to carry on His work with confidence – "to seek and to save that which was lost" (Luke 19:10). He gave you a clear command and empowered you to go and continue the work He came to do! While it may not always make sense to you, your job, as an athlete of God, is to trust and obey! Therefore, run the race faithfully today and execute the play of the day for the glory of God.

Day 29 Promise 29
The Promise of Completion

1) Know God's Playbook. The play of the day is Philippians 1:6:

"For I am confident of this very thing, that He who began a good work in you will perfect it until the day of Christ Jesus."

2) Train for Godliness. The invitation of God for you today is to learn to trust that God is at work in you to do what He says He will do. Your calling is to work with Him according to His promise!

"So then, my beloved, just as you have always obeyed, not as in my presence only, but now much more in my absence, work out your salvation with fear and trembling; for it is God who is at work in you, both to will and to work for His good pleasure" (Philippians 2:12-13).

Confidence is a determination to act! It is a conviction you have trained into your head and heart. When I was training for the 2000 Olympics, I was confident in my training regimen so that, as I competed on some of the biggest stages of my sport, I was able to do so at the highest level and win the victory.

"Do you not know that those who run in a race all run, but only one receives the prize? Run in such a way that you may win. Everyone who competes in the games exercises self-control in all things. They then do it to receive a perishable wreath, but we an imperishable"
(1 Corinthians 9:24-25).

3) Listen to the Coach. As I have known, trained with, and competed against some of the world's best in my sport, I often think of the sacrifices each of those athletes made to achieve their level of athletic success. Every one of them is a champion, even when they don't act, sound, or look like it. So often, our greatest ministry is found in our faithful and hopeful mindset through the painful training regimen of everyday life. We stay the course because we trust the Coach, and we are convinced that the prize is worth it.

**"For I consider that the sufferings of this present time are not worthy
to be compared with the glory that is to be revealed to us"
(Romans 8:18).**

God's promise of completion teaches us that even if there are times
you don't act like a champion, you still are one. You don't have to be
perfect – that's God's job! Your calling is to press on to the prize; so take
the next step and don't quit!

**"Brethren, I do not regard myself as having laid hold of it yet; but one
thing I do: forgetting what lies behind and reaching forward to what
lies ahead, I press on toward the goal for the prize of the upward call
of God in Christ Jesus" (Philippians 3:13-14).**

4) Work together with God's team. God invites you into partnership with
Him, not to take over for Him. Just as you could not begin with Christ
apart from the work of the Holy Spirit, you cannot be brought to maturity
in Christ without the ministry of the Holy Spirit (Galatians 3:3).

**"I thank my God always concerning you for the grace of God which
was given you in Christ Jesus, that in everything you were enriched in
Him, in all speech and all knowledge, even as the testimony
concerning Christ was confirmed in you, so that you are not lacking
in any gift, awaiting eagerly the revelation of our Lord Jesus Christ,
who will also confirm you to the end, blameless in the day of our Lord
Jesus Christ" (1 Corinthians 1:4-8).**

Trust God and partner in the work He is doing in and through you.
God not only promises to complete His work in you, but also to provide
for the work He has invited you to do with Him, every step of your race.
Therefore, run the race faithfully today and execute the play of the day for
the glory of God.

Day 30 Promise 30
The Promise of Fruitfulness

1) Know God's Playbook. The play of the day is John 15:5:

"I am the vine, you are the branches; he who abides in Me and I in him, he bears much fruit, for apart from Me you can do nothing."

2) Train for Godliness. Bearing fruit is all about faith, not works! It is God who bears fruit on our branch when we learn to abide (connect, remain) with Jesus Christ. You can work for Jesus and have good intentions, but apart from Him you will do nothing of eternal value. That's a promise!

"And without faith it is impossible to please Him, for he who comes to God must believe that He is and that He is a rewarder of those who seek Him" (Hebrews 11:6).

We develop a rhythm of faith habits by building a rule of life, or "trellis," for our allotment of seeds (Romans 12:3) to grow. A trellis is the agricultural image of a wooden framework by which a fruit tree or vine is supported, so that it grows and bears fruit. Because we don't want our faith to lay fallow in the field, or rot on the ground, we build a trellis for it to grow and become fruitful. A rule of life incorporates your personal spiritual disciplines and faith community practices that strengthen your spiritual vitality by framing your life in the unforced rhythms of grace. It's your training regimen!

"Either make the tree good and its fruit good, or make the tree bad and its fruit bad; for the tree is known by its fruit. ... The good man brings out of his good treasure what is good; and the evil man brings out of his evil treasure what is evil" (Matthew 12:33-35).

3) Listen to the Coach. As part of becoming a fruitful athlete on God's team, we are to prioritize our abiding time with Jesus – Bible intake and prayer! One of the keystone habits of my rule of life is to prioritize time abiding with Jesus at the beginning of my day.

"In the early morning, while it was still dark, Jesus got up, left the house, and went away to a secluded place, and was praying there" (Mark 1:35).

Practically, when I first wake up, I read my Bible and pray before I turn on my phone or look at any media. To do this faithfully, I must wake up earlier than my family, which means that I must protect my evening times so that I wake up rested and ready to listen to the Coach before I start running plays of my own initiative, or under my own power. This practice forms my day, because the unforced rhythms of grace are shaping my mind and heart from the starting block!

4) Work together with God's team. Jesus invites us to bear fruit with Him by praying with Him on a regular basis in set apart ways, as was His custom.

"And He came out and proceeded as was His custom to the Mount of Olives; and the disciples also followed Him. When He arrived at the place, He said to them, 'Pray that you may not enter into temptation.' And He withdrew from them about a stone's throw, and He knelt down and began to pray, saying, 'Father, if You are willing, remove this cup from Me; yet not My will, but Yours be done'" (Luke 22:39-42).

Make this a rhythm of grace in your life so that you may experience God's presence and power from the beginning to the end of your day. When you begin and end your day with God, then your trellis is facilitating the growth potential to be able to "pray without ceasing" (1 Thessalonians 5:17). Such fruitfulness does not happen by accident! It is by applying diligence to the promise of fruitfulness that you will focus on abiding in the Vine, and with the Holy Spirit coursing through your branch that you will bear much fruit and prove to be His athlete (John 15:7-8). Therefore, run the race faithfully today and execute the play of the day for the glory of God.

Day 31 Promise 31
The Promise of Tribulations

1) Know God's Playbook. The play of the day is Romans 5:3-5:

"And not only this, but we also exult in our tribulations, knowing that tribulation brings about perseverance; and perseverance, proven character; and proven character, hope; and hope does not disappoint, because the love of God has been poured out within our hearts through the Holy Spirit who was given to us."

2) Train for Godliness. Every athlete knows that hard days (seasons) will come; sickness and injuries do happen, setbacks in training occur, and disappointments are common in competitions. Only an inexperienced athlete believes that he or she will not get hurt or have a slump. The key is not to bail before the blessing!

"Consider it all joy, my brethren, when you encounter various trials, knowing that the testing of your faith produces endurance. And let endurance have its perfect result, so that you may be perfect and complete, lacking in nothing" (James 1:2-4).

In the 2000 US Olympic Track and Field Team Trials, I had one last throw to move into the top three to accomplish my goal and make the team. For years I had trained with my coach, Dr. Greg Gassner, and my sports psychologist, Dr. Nate Zinsser, on approaching each throw as an opportunity to have confidence and trust my training. That day, my years of training, day in and day out, paid off and I had my best throw in my final effort and moved into third place. This doesn't happen by accident in sports, or in our everyday lives. God's athletes must train a mindset of perseverance to the finish line. Finishing strong is a trained mindset!

"I have fought the good fight, I have finished the course, I have kept the faith" (2 Timothy 4:7).

3) Listen to the Coach. Every crisis is an opportunity to grow in character! God's athletes must train themselves to trust God in every circumstance and respond in faith. This is how you live like a champion today!

"As an example, brethren, of suffering and patience, take the prophets who spoke in the name of the Lord. We count those blessed who endured. You have heard of the endurance of Job and have seen the outcome of the Lord's dealings, that the Lord is full of compassion and is merciful" (James 5:10-11).

The Lord teaches us that we are to trust Him in every situation because He will give us the way of escape so that we can be transformed into Christlikeness through our response. God's promise of tribulations comes with the victory of our faith!

"No temptation has overtaken you but such as is common to man; and God is faithful, who will not allow you to be tempted beyond what you are able, but with the temptation will provide the way of escape also, so that you will be able to endure it" (1 Corinthians 10:13).

4) Work together with God's team. In Jesus' final words to the seven churches of Revelation, there is one character quality of the saints that is rewarded every time: Perseverance!

"To him who overcomes, I will grant to eat of the tree of life which is in the Paradise of God" (Revelation 2:7; cf. 2:11, 17; 26-28; 3:5, 12, 21).

"For whatever is born of God overcomes the world; and this is the victory that has overcome the world – our faith" (1 John 5:4).

You are an overcomer! This is the good fruit of the promise of tribulation. When you face hardship with faith, perseverance forges character, and character produces hope, and hope never disappoints because it is the Holy Spirit who perseveres in every athlete of God. Therefore, run the race faithfully today and execute the play of the day for the glory of God.

Day 32 Promise 32
The Promise of Representing

1) Know God's Playbook. The play of the day is Ephesians 5:20:

"Therefore, we are ambassadors for Christ, as though God were making an appeal through us; we beg you on behalf of Christ, be reconciled to God."

2) Train for Godliness. When Christ returns on the Day of His royal visitation there will no longer be a need for us to be His ambassadors, but until that Day we are His authorized representatives here in the many outposts of Earth called churches, far from His heavenly home. Therefore, we are to ensure that our lives represent Him and His Kingdom, not ourselves or the monuments we so desire to erect in our own names.

"But examine everything carefully; hold fast to that which is good; abstain from every form of evil. Now may the God of peace Himself sanctify you entirely; and may your spirit and soul and body be preserved complete, without blame at the coming of our Lord Jesus Christ. Faithful is He who calls you, and He also will bring it to pass" (1 Thessalonians 5:21-24).

What an amazing truth – God is making His appeal through you! God has taken your life and your story and is transforming it to tell a better story – the gospel of Jesus Christ! He has placed His treasure in you for His glory! It is the treasure in you – God's glory – and not you, the vessel, that the world needs to see, so live like a champion today and make Him known by shining God's light into the darkness.

"For God, who said, 'Light shall shine out of darkness,' is the One who has shone in our hearts to give the Light of the knowledge of the glory of God in the face of Christ. But we have this treasure in earthen vessels, so that the surpassing greatness of the power will be of God and not from ourselves" (2 Corinthians 4:6-7).

3) Listen to the Coach. Jesus commands us to go about the work of God until He returns. We are His authorized witnesses of His Kingdom, and workers of His vineyard, until the Lord Jesus returns. You are invited to do the work of the King and represent His voice until He returns.

> **"A nobleman went to a distant country to receive a kingdom for himself, and then return. And he called ten of his slaves, and gave them ten minas and said to them, 'Do business with this until I come back'"** (Luke 19:12-13).

> **"It is not for you to know times or epochs which the Father has fixed by His own authority; but you will receive power when the Holy Spirit has come upon you; and you shall be My witnesses both in Jerusalem, and in all Judea and Samaria, and even to the remotest part of the earth"** (Acts 1:7-8).

4) Work together with God's team. As an athlete, I had the privilege of representing the USA in Croatia and Spain. What an honor! We are called to serve as ambassadors in many different places throughout the world, as members of the same team. God's team is the body of Christ; we put Him on display for all to see and know Him.

> **"With all prayer and petition pray at all times in the Spirit, and with this in view, be on the alert with all perseverance and petition for all the saints, and pray on my behalf, that utterance may be given to me in the opening of my mouth, to make known with boldness the mystery of the gospel, for which I am an ambassador in chains; that in proclaiming it I may speak boldly, as I ought to speak"** (Ephesians 6:18-20).

As members of God's team, we are invited to pray for and encourage one another. Together, we are the body of Christ, and we may be the only Jesus some people ever see or hear. Therefore, run the race faithfully today and execute the play of the day for the glory of God.

Day 33 Promise 33
The Promise of Stillness

1) Know God's Playbook. The play of the day is Psalm 46:10:

"Cease striving and know that I am God; I will be exalted among the nations, I will be exalted in the earth."

2) Train for Godliness. The play of the day is a difficult part of the training regimen for many of God's athletes. It is the spiritual discipline of silence and solitude – to be still by ceasing from work and *intending* your attention on the presence of God!

"But the LORD is in His holy temple. Let all the earth be silent before Him" (Habakkuk 2:20).

The hard truth of this promise in today's frenetic "25/8" culture is that the promise of stillness requires us to disconnect from the feeds, videos, and all else that has captured our attentions and intentions, to experience the rhythm of being still. We are to *intend* our attention on the presence of God during times of silence and solitude!

"Be silent before the Lord GOD! For the day of the LORD is near, For the LORD has prepared a sacrifice, He has consecrated His guests" (Zephaniah 1:7).

Prioritize time today to sit in silence for twenty minutes and experience what happens to you and where your attention goes. No radio or tv, no background noise, no active study or message, no scheming or planning, just a solitary focus on God and His promised presence.

3) Listen to the Coach. We are hyper-connected, yet many of us are lonely; we are over-committed, yet many of us are bored. We love our activism (religious, political, economic, entertainment, etc.), yet our souls languish from the drought and exhaustion of not being still before God. We are too focused on our own important plans and activities to prioritize and protect intentional times of tending to our souls through the promise of stillness. When we meet with God, we are reminded that He will be exalted among the nations. We are too busy exalting ourselves and our opinions to prioritize time to sit at Jesus' feet and listen to Him and His Word.

"But Martha was distracted with all her preparations; and she came up to Him and said, 'Lord, do You not care that my sister has left me to do all the serving alone? Then tell her to help me.' But the Lord answered and said to her, 'Martha, Martha, you are worried and bothered about so many things; but only one thing is necessary, for Mary has chosen the good part, which shall not be taken away from her'" (Luke 10:40-42).

It is in these times and places that God reveals to us the truth about ourselves, and how "worried and bothered" we are by so many things. Be still in His loving embrace and remember who He is, and who you are in Him.

4) Work together with God's team. Jesus *intended* His attention on the presence of God throughout His ministry. He prayed at His baptism (Luke 3:21) and then immediately went off for a prolonged forty days of silence and solitude in the wilderness (Luke 4:1-2). Jesus gave Himself to the Cross after a time of being still before the Lord, as was His custom, in the Garden of Gethsemane.

"And He came out and proceeded as was His custom to the Mount of Olives; and the disciples also followed Him. When He arrived at the place, He said to them, 'Pray that you may not enter into temptation.' And He withdrew from them about a stone's throw, and He knelt down and began to pray, saying, 'Father, if You are willing, remove this cup from Me; yet not My will, but Yours be done'" (Luke 22:39-42).

The Coach invites you, His athlete, to come away with Him and learn from the example of His Son, so that the Father's will would be accomplished, first in you, then through you. Therefore, run the race faithfully today and execute the play of the day for the glory of God.

Day 34 Promise 34
The Promise of Waiting

1) Know God's Playbook. The play of the day is Isaiah 40:31:

"Yet those who wait for the LORD will gain new strength; they will mount up with wings like eagles, they will run and not get tired, they will walk and not become weary."

2) Train for Godliness. Patience is a fruit of the Spirit (Galatians 5:22) and an essential ingredient in the discipleship journey for every athlete of God. Your conformity to Christ is a long slow obedience in the same direction that requires you to wait upon the Lord, learning His goodness and grace in every circumstance of life. Don't bail before the blessing, and never quit – the reward is in the patience!

"The LORD is good to those who wait for Him, to the person who seeks Him. It is good that he waits silently for the salvation of the LORD" (Lamentations 3:25-26).

One of my greatest failures as an athlete was at the 1996 NCAA Division 1 Track & Field Championships. I was the top-ranked American collegiate hammer thrower and was facing the soon-to-be Olympic gold medalist from Hungary, a student at USC. I was in the best shape of my life, and was throwing far in the warm-ups, but even my best was far short of Balázs Kiss' world-leading throws. In one of the most painful learning experiences of my athletic life, I let a competitor in my head, and I lost my patience; I rushed my first throw and sector fouled. Instead of letting the adrenaline do its job, I overstimulated my system and had my worst competition of my senior year on the biggest collegiate platform. While my impatience had catastrophic effects on my performance (and pride!) that day, there are much greater consequences to not running the play of the day in real life. I learned a valuable lesson and had an excellent meet a month later at the 1996 USA Track & Field Olympic Team Trials in Atlanta, Georgia, even up against Lance Deal, the soon-to-be Olympic silver medalist. I remained patient and was rewarded for it!

"Wait for the LORD; be strong and let your heart take courage; yes, wait for the LORD" (Psalm 27:14).

3) Listen to the Coach. You are invited to prioritize waiting upon God for wisdom and discernment as you seek to hear God's voice and run the right play at the right time. The athletes of God are to wait on God for His direction. Jesus modeled this for us. Prior to making the big decision of who His twelve apostles would be, Jesus waited upon God, in prayer, for His Father's direction.

"It was at this time that He went off to the mountain to pray, and He spent the whole night in prayer to God" (Luke 6:12).

"I wait for the LORD, my soul does wait, and in His word do I hope" (Psalm 130:5).

4) Work together with God's team. We are to learn from Jesus' example and wait upon the Lord for His strength, and His direction, in all that we set out to accomplish. We may not understand God's timing, or purposes, in our waiting, but we can know that His ways are for our good and will bring about His victory, in and through our lives. This was true in the death and resuscitation of Lazarus, which Jesus declared would be for God's glory before and after calling Lazarus forth.

"But when Jesus heard this, He said, 'This sickness is not to end in death, but for the glory of God, so that the Son of God may be glorified by it.' … Jesus said to her, 'Did I not say to you that if you believe, you will see the glory of God?'" (John 11:4, 40).

Often, it is our impatience that gets in the way of God's victory being manifested in and through our lives and circumstances. The athletes of God are called to wait upon the Lord, trust the Coach's play book, and trust His timing and direction. Therefore, run the race faithfully today and execute the play of the day for the glory of God.

Day 35 Promise 35
The Promise of Comfort

1) Know God's Playbook. The play of the day is 2 Corinthians 1:3-4:

"Blessed be the God and Father of our Lord Jesus Christ, the Father of mercies and God of all comfort, who comforts us in all our affliction so that we will be able to comfort those who are in any affliction with the comfort with which we ourselves are comforted by God."

2) Train for Godliness. To comfort means to alleviate sorrow, to relieve distress, to give emotional strength. To comfort someone is an activity of love from one person to another. God incarnates this promise to us, and then between us, from one person to another! An everyday example of this is the comfort of a mother.

"Surely I have composed and quieted my soul; like a weaned child rests against his mother, my soul is like a weaned child within me" (Psalm 131:2).

"But we proved to be gentle among you, as a nursing mother tenderly cares for her own children. Having so fond an affection for you, we were well-pleased to impart to you not only the gospel of God but also our own lives, because you had become very dear to us" (1 Thessalonians 2:7-8).

This is the gospel ministry of Jesus Christ through men and women alike. We are to extend to one another the same nurture and love, the same compassion and mercy, the same gentleness and grace, as a mother to her child. This is the love that God first gave us, and this is the love that will transform the world through His athletes who are trained according to this promise. Jesus was "moved by compassion" and we are to be, too (Matthew 9:36).

3) Listen to the Coach. The Holy Spirit administers this comfort by mediating the presence of God directly to you and through you. You are now the one who is to bring God's comfort to others – in the same way that you have been comforted, now comfort others!

- God reached from Heaven to Earth through the incarnation of Jesus Christ to comfort you, now pick up the phone, or send a card, to comfort another.
- Jesus died on the Cross to comfort you, now make a meal and deliver it to someone to comfort them.
- Jesus defeated death in the resurrection to comfort you, now show up and visit someone to comfort them.
- Jesus has ascended to the right hand of the Father and is coming again to comfort us, now leave the comfort of your own home to help your neighbor in need.
- The Holy Spirit comforts you as your constant companion, now use words that comfort the clerks in stores, waitresses in restaurants, and those you interact with daily.

4) Work together with God's team. God incarnates His promise of comfort! The promise of comfort, like all the promises of God, is found in Jesus Christ. It is the gift of God to His people – this is God's magnificent salvation to bring us the comfort Isaiah prophesied.

"'Comfort, O comfort My people,' says your God. 'Speak kindly to Jerusalem; and call out to her, that her warfare has ended, that her iniquity has been removed, that she has received of the LORD's hand double for all her sins.' A voice is calling, 'Clear the way for the LORD in the wilderness; make smooth in the desert a highway for our God'" (Isaiah 40:1-3).

The promise of comfort is so important in the lives of God's people, especially when we face disease and death, darkness and despair, disappointment in this life, and defeat at the hands of our enemies. You need comfort when the scoreboard at halftime looks desperate, but there is still plenty of time to play! You need light in this darkness, hope in this despair, healing from this disease, and deliverance from death! Comfort allows you to live like a champion today by playing the game according to the promises of God! Therefore, run the race faithfully today and execute the play of the day for the glory of God.

Day 36 Promise 36
The Promise of Serving

1) Know God's Playbook. The play of the day is John 13:15-17:

"For I gave you an example that you also should do as I did to you. Truly, truly, I say to you, a slave is not greater than his master, nor is one who is sent greater than the one who sent him. If you know these things, you are blessed if you do them."

2) Train for Godliness. To be Jesus' apprentice, you are to copy what the master does; but this will become a heavy burden if it doesn't flow out of the transformation of your character through the renewal of your mind (Romans 12:2). Jesus didn't serve the disciples by washing their feet so that they would feel entitled. While entitlement is a huge issue in our culture, it should never be an issue for someone who is following in the footsteps of Jesus Christ!

As the Lord and Teacher, Jesus washed His disciples' feet to show His current and future disciples the new way of life. This is the life of love and service, flowing not from our flesh, but from the emptying of our flesh and the infilling of the Holy Spirit who empowers our lives in Christ. This is the example of Jesus, and the way to live like a champion today.

"Do nothing from selfishness or empty conceit, but with humility of mind regard one another as more important than yourselves; do not merely look out for your own personal interests, but also for the interests of others. Have this attitude in yourselves which was also in Christ Jesus, who, although He existed in the form of God, did not regard equality with God a thing to be grasped, but emptied Himself, taking the form of a bond-servant, and being made in the likeness of men. Being found in appearance as a man, He humbled Himself by becoming obedient to the point of death, even death on a cross"
(Philippians 2:3-8).

3) Listen to the Coach. The body of Christ is composed of many individual members; we can only fit together and work together when we each follow the example of Jesus.

"You know that the rulers of the Gentiles lord it over them, and their great men exercise authority over them. It is not this way among you, but whoever wishes to become great among you shall be your servant, and whoever wishes to be first among you shall be your slave; just as the Son of Man did not come to be served, but to serve, and to give His life a ransom for many" (Matthew 20:25-28).

The Lord set an example, not only in washing the feet of His disciples on the night He was betrayed, but in demonstrating the ultimate example of a servant by taking our sins upon Himself on the Cross of Calvary and giving us His right relationship with the Father (2 Corinthians 5:21).

4) Work together with God's team. God's athletes are to live a life of service, from the inside out. The promise of service comes with the invitation to humble yourself and live for a different audience than the world provides. God's athletes serve to hear these words from Jesus: "Well done, good and faithful servant" (Matthew 25:23).

"Whatever you do, do your work heartily, as for the Lord rather than for men, knowing that from the Lord you will receive the reward of the inheritance. It is the Lord Christ whom you serve" (Colossians 3:23-24).

You may think that the practice of serving would be to serve; while that is the outcome, the ultimate spiritual discipline is to think more highly of others than you think of yourself, and serve them as Christ first served you – being "gentle and humble in heart" (Matthew 11:29). Therefore, run the race faithfully today and execute the play of the day for the glory of God.

Day 37 Promise 37
The Promise of Abundance

1) Know God's Playbook. The play of the day is 2 Corinthians 9:8:

"God is able to make all grace abound to you, so that always having all sufficiency in everything, you may have an abundance for every good deed."

2) Train for Godliness. God always provides for that which He promises. This is a spiritual axiom because God cannot lie. If Paul says that God will provide in abundance for every good deed, then it is done. The abundant life is Jesus' desire for your life as a member of God's team. There is an enemy to your soul that would have you distrust God's promises and act out of your insecurity and fear; train yourself to trust God's Word and live according to your faith – live like a champion today!

"The thief comes only to steal and kill and destroy; I came that they may have life, and have it abundantly" (John 10:10).

Neither Jesus' promise in John 10:10, nor Paul's in 2 Corinthians 9:8, protects you from the reality of living in a fallen world: there will be natural disasters, financial hardships, medical crises, relational strains, and vocational uncertainties. That is just real life! The abundant life is the life of God's sufficient grace, and it means that God's provision is up to the challenge you are called to endure.

"And He has said to me, 'My grace is sufficient for you, for power is perfected in weakness.' Most gladly, therefore, I will rather boast about my weaknesses, so that the power of Christ may dwell in me. Therefore I am well content with weaknesses, with insults, with distresses, with persecutions, with difficulties, for Christ's sake; for when I am weak, then I am strong" (2 Corinthians 12:9-10).

3) Listen to the Coach. The way to experiencing the abundance of God is by building your life upon God's Word. Jesus concluded the Sermon on the Mount by contrasting two foundations for your life – shifting sand or solid rock (Matthew 7:24-27). If you want to experience the promise of abundance, then you must build your life upon obedience to God's Word, the solid rock. This is the prosperity of your soul!

"This book of the law shall not depart from your mouth, but you shall meditate on it day and night, so that you may be careful to do according to all that is written in it; for then you will make your way prosperous, and then you will have success" (Joshua 1:8).

"How blessed is the man who does not walk in the counsel of the wicked, nor stand in the path of sinners, nor sit in the seat of scoffers! But his delight is in the law of the LORD, and in His law he meditates day and night. He will be like a tree firmly planted by streams of water, which yields its fruit in its season and its leaf does not wither; and in whatever he does, he prospers" (Psalm 1:1-3).

4) Work together with God's team. Be generous with your time, talents, and treasures. Don't hold back what God has so richly bestowed upon you!

"Now this I say, he who sows sparingly will also reap sparingly, and he who sows bountifully will also reap bountifully. Each one must do just as he has purposed in his heart, not grudgingly or under compulsion, for God loves a cheerful giver" (2 Corinthians 9:6-7).

God's team prospers as each team member prospers! Jesus teaches us that "it is more blessed to give than to receive," so be generous with all that God has bestowed on you (Acts 20:35). The way God provides for His promise is by each member of the team excelling at doing his or her part. Therefore, run the race faithfully today and execute the play of the day for the glory of God.

Day 38 Promise 38
The Promise of Conforming to His Image

1) Know God's Playbook. The play of the day is Romans 8:29-30:

"For those whom He foreknew, He also predestined to become conformed to the image of His Son, so that He would be the firstborn among many brethren; and these whom He predestined, He also called; and these whom He called, He also justified; and these whom He justified, He also glorified."

2) Train for Godliness. From the beginning, it was God's glory to create us in His image. He created us to join with Him in His work to bring order to the chaos and fill the void with His goodness. God's original design for you was to be a partaker of His divine nature (2 Peter 1:4)!

"God created man in His own image, in the image of God He created him; male and female He created them. God blessed them; and God said to them, be fruitful and multiply, and fill the earth, and subdue it; and rule over the fish of the sea and over the birds of the sky and over every living thing that moves on the earth" (Genesis 1:27-28).

Jesus came to restore us back to God's image, that we might partner with Him in His great rescue plan to the bless the nations. So, while your glorification with God is a future hope that will not be perfected until the Day of Christ Jesus (Philippians 1:6), God's glory has already come to you in love, so that you can know Jesus and become more like Him!

"He came to His own, and those who were His own did not receive Him. But as many as received Him, to them He gave the right to become children of God, even to those who believe in His name, who were born, not of blood nor of the will of the flesh nor of the will of man, but of God. And the Word became flesh, and dwelt among us, and we saw His glory, glory as of the only begotten from the Father, full of grace and truth" (John 1:11-14).

3) Listen to the Coach. Every arena of your life comes under the purview of this promise. You serve God best when you walk in conformity to His character as revealed in Jesus Christ (Colossians 2:9-10). Jesus prayed this for all His followers.

"The glory which You have given Me I have given to them, that they may be one, just as We are one; I in them and You in Me, that they may be perfected in unity, so that the world may know that You sent Me, and loved them, even as You have loved Me. Father, I desire that they also, whom You have given Me, be with Me where I am, so that they may see My glory which You have given Me, for You loved Me before the foundation of the world" (John 17:22-24).

4) Work together with God's team. Paul had an earnest expectation of this hope and devoted His ambition to it.

"More than that, I count all things to be loss in view of the surpassing value of knowing Christ Jesus my Lord, for whom I have suffered the loss of all things, and count them but rubbish so that I may gain Christ, and may be found in Him, not having a righteousness of my own derived from the Law, but that which is through faith in Christ, the righteousness which comes from God on the basis of faith, that I may know Him and the power of His resurrection and the fellowship of His sufferings, being conformed to His death; in order that I may attain to the resurrection from the dead" (Philippians 3:8-11).

Until every member of the team is working for the same ambition, in every circumstance, our disunity will keep us from manifesting the victory that is ours in Christ Jesus. Focus your heart and mind on God's transforming work of your soul, so that you, too, will be conformed to His image. Therefore, run the race faithfully today and execute the play of the day for the glory of God.

Day 39 Promise 39
The Promise of Joy

1) Know God's Playbook. The play of the day is John 15:11:

"These things I have spoken to you so that My joy may be in you, and that your joy may be made full."

2) Train for Godliness. God's desire is that you may experience the fullness of Jesus' joy in you, and that His joy would complete your joy. It was for this reason that Jesus Christ went to the Cross.

"Fixing our eyes on Jesus, the author and perfecter of faith, who for the joy set before Him endured the cross, despising the shame, and has sat down at the right hand of the throne of God. For consider Him who has endured such hostility by sinners against Himself, so that you will not grow weary and lose heart" (Hebrews 12:2-3).

Nehemiah declared in Nehemiah 8:10, "The joy of the LORD is your strength." Eric Liddell, the famous Christian athlete from the 1981 movie *Chariots of Fire*, said that, when he ran, he experienced the pleasure of God. We, too, can run the race set before us in the same way Jesus faced the Cross and Eric Liddell chased Olympic gold – for the joy set before us! In fact, for the Christian athlete, joy is a daily discipline of the training regimen! No matter the circumstance or challenge, we are commanded to rejoice in the Lord.

"Rejoice in the Lord always; again I will say, rejoice"
(Philippians 4:4)!

3) Listen to the Coach. It is to the fulfillment of the promise of joy from John 15:11 that John, the Beloved of Jesus, wrote his powerful first letter.

"These things we write, so that our joy may be made complete"
(1 John 1:4).

Joy is the work of the Holy Spirit in our lives; it is not a product of our flesh or our circumstances. It is a manifestation of the will of God, in us and through us, so that the world may come to know God's love through Jesus Christ.

"But the fruit of the Spirit is love, joy, peace, patience, kindness, goodness, faithfulness, gentleness, self-control; against such things there is no law. Now those who belong to Christ Jesus have crucified the flesh with its passions and desires. If we live by the Spirit, let us also walk by the Spirit" (Galatians 5:22-25).

"Rejoice always; pray without ceasing; in everything give thanks; for this is God's will for you in Christ Jesus" (1 Thessalonians 5:16-18).

4) Work together with God's team. We are to share our joy with one another! Joy motivates us to live the sacrificial and generous life of a Christian athlete.

"But even if I am being poured out as a drink offering upon the sacrifice and service of your faith, I rejoice and share my joy with you all. You too, I urge you, rejoice in the same way and share your joy with me" (Philippians 2:17-18).

"For even though I am absent in body, nevertheless I am with you in spirit, rejoicing to see your good discipline and the stability of your faith in Christ" (Colossians 2:5).

"Now, brethren, we wish to make known to you the grace of God which has been given in the churches of Macedonia, that in a great ordeal of affliction their abundance of joy and their deep poverty overflowed in the wealth of their liberality" (2 Corinthians 8:1-2).

When we live out of the abundance of the joy Jesus gives us, then we live faithfully according to the Coach's vision for His team. Therefore, run the race faithfully today and execute the play of the day for the glory of God.

Day 40 Promise 40
The Promise of Love

1) Know God's Playbook. The play of the day is 1 John 3:1-2:

"See how great a love the Father has bestowed on us, that we would be called children of God; and such we are. For this reason the world does not know us, because it did not know Him. Beloved, now we are children of God, and it has not appeared as yet what we will be. We know that when He appears, we will be like Him, because we will see Him just as He is."

2) Train for Godliness. Jesus taught us love by intentionally turning the world upside down with the love of God. Jesus ushered in the Kingdom of God when He, the conquering King, came through the virgin womb of a teenage bride, in opposition to the powers and principalities of this world (Luke 1:26-38; 2:1-20).

Jesus invites you to turn the world upside down by loving and living like He did – as a witness of His upside-down Kingdom; He defeated the principalities and powers of this world, by allowing them to crucify Him upon the Cross (Philippians 2:5-11). This is the way of God's love! This is our victory!

"God so loved the world, that He gave His only begotten Son, that whoever believes in Him shall not perish, but have eternal life. For God did not send the Son into the world to judge the world, but that the world might be saved through Him" (John 3:16-17).

3) Listen to the Coach. We are eagerly awaiting Jesus' second royal visitation, when His love will complete that which has already been begun in us (Philippians 1:6). Until that Day, you are called to love others as God first loved you (Romans 5:8). Live like a champion today!

"A new commandment I give to you, that you love one another, even as I have loved you, that you also love one another. By this all men will know that you are My disciples, if you have love for one another" (John 13:34-35).

"Beloved, let us love one another, for love is from God; and everyone who loves is born of God and knows God. The one who does not love does not know God, for God is love. By this the love of God was manifested in us, that God has sent His only begotten Son into the world so that we might live through Him. In this is love, not that we loved God, but that He loved us and sent His Son to be the propitiation for our sins. Beloved, if God so loved us, we also ought to love one another" (1 John 4:7-11).

4) Work together with God's team. We are more than conquerors through Him who loved us because the victory is a vicarious one, meaning that it is a victory bestowed on us, not one we earned (Romans 8:37). It is because of God's love, not our own, that we have been set free from sin to live for God (1 John 4:10).

"There is no fear in love; but perfect love casts out fear, because fear involves punishment, and the one who fears is not perfected in love. We love, because He first loved us. If someone says, 'I love God,' and hates his brother, he is a liar; for the one who does not love his brother whom he has seen, cannot love God whom he has not seen. And this commandment we have from Him, that the one who loves God should love his brother also" (1 John 4:18-21).

Teammates must practice this play with one another; if you are not loving, you are missing the whole point (John 14:15, 21, 23). Relationships are not just a play in the playbook, they are God's strategy for the whole playbook. This is the banner over God's Team – LOVE! We are the beloved of God, chosen and called to show the world His love. Therefore, run the race faithfully today and execute the play of the day for the glory of God.

Dr. Jerry D. Ingalls

SECTION 3

THE PRECIOUS AND MAGNIFICENT

PROMISES OF GOD!

In our lives we don't speak readily of victory. It is too big a word
for us. We have suffered too many defeats in our lives; victory
has been thwarted again and again by too many weak hours, too
many gross sins. But isn't it true that the spirit within us yearns
for this word, for the final victory over the sin and anxious fear
of death in our lives? And now God's word also says nothing to
us about our victory; it doesn't promise us that we will be
victorious over sin and death from now own [sic]; rather, it says
with all its might that someone has won this victory, and that this
person, if we have him as Lord, will also win the victory over us.
It is not we who are victorious, but Jesus.[5]

---

5 Dietrich Bonhoeffer, *God Is in the Manger: Reflections on Advent and Christmas*,
ed. Jana Riess, trans. O. C. Dean Jr., First edition (Louisville, KY: Westminster
John Knox Press, 2010), 75.

Dr. Jerry D. Ingalls

Chapter 3
The Promise of Being on God's Team

Grace and peace be multiplied to you in the knowledge of God and of Jesus our Lord; seeing that His divine power has granted to us everything pertaining to life and godliness, through the true knowledge of Him who called us by His own glory and excellence. For by these He has granted to us His precious and magnificent promises, so that by them you may become partakers of the divine nature, having escaped the corruption that is in the world by lust.
2 Peter 1:3-4

This section's quote comes from Dietrich Bonhoeffer, who, at the end of 1939, explained this critical truth in his "Christus Victor" address: the victory we live is a vicarious one.

The key to all the promises of God is found in Bonhoeffer's words, "if we have him as Lord, [Jesus] will also win the victory over us." The victory we have, and the victory we live, is a vicarious one. That means it is a victory that is not of our own making or doing, but rather a victory that has been given to us through the life, death, and resurrection of Jesus Christ. It is something we are privileged to "partake" in or share.

Living like a champion today is, and will always be, God's work of grace in us and through us for His glory! Let us be clear about this from the forefront: it's all grace!

Paul said in 2 Corinthians 1:20-22, "For as many as are the promises of God, in Him they are yes; therefore also through Him is our Amen to the glory of God through us. Now He who establishes us with you in Christ and anointed us is God, who also sealed us and gave us the Spirit in our hearts as a pledge."

Your faith is a received faith, not a created one. You have received a faith of the same kind as Paul's, by the righteousness of our God and Savior, Jesus Christ. Grace and peace are multiplied to you through the knowledge of God, and of Jesus our Lord, because He has granted to us everything pertaining to life and godliness through His divine power.

Peter made it very clear from the very beginning: God has granted to you His precious and magnificent promises – they are all of grace so that by God's promises you may become partakers of the divine nature, having escaped the corruption that is in the world by lust.

God has given you victory through His precious and magnificent promises, and that victory is your fellowship in the Trinity – you are alive in Christ, no longer cut off or dead in sin! You have been delivered and rescued; now, God is calling you to live through His divine nature – to live in the victory of Jesus Christ! His victory is found in every promise of God that has been lavishly poured out upon you through your adoption as sons, the children of God with right of inheritance. Paul explains this miracle of grace in Galatians 4:4-7:

> But when the fullness of the time came, God sent forth His Son, born of a woman, born under the Law, so that He might redeem those who were under the Law, that we might receive the adoption as sons. Because you are sons, God has sent forth the Spirit of His Son into our hearts, crying, "Abba! Father!" Therefore you are no longer a slave, but a son; and if a son, then an heir through God.

You are an heir to all the promises of God! You will be His people and He will be your God! As Paul proclaims of our rich inheritance in Ephesians 2:4-10:

But God, being rich in mercy, because of His great love with which He loved us, even when we were dead in our transgressions, made us alive together with Christ (by grace you have been saved), and raised us up with Him, and seated us with Him in the heavenly places in Christ Jesus, so that in the ages to come He might show the surpassing riches of His grace in kindness toward us in Christ Jesus. For by grace, you have been saved through faith; and that not of yourselves, it is the gift of God; not as a result of works, so that no one may boast. For we are His workmanship, created in Christ Jesus for good works, which God prepared beforehand so that we would walk in them.

It's as if you already have been fitted for your championship ring, now you just need to trust that the victory is yours and live like a champion and wait for the day when the ring is put on your finger. It is done!

The promises of God are both a future-focused faith (hope) and a present practice of faith. Partaking in God's nature is both a promise of immortality (eternal life, salvation, born again, etc.), and also the life of a new morality (Christlikeness, godliness, righteousness, holiness, etc.).

In Romans 6:4-5, Paul taught us this is the meaning of our baptism, the imagery of our being united in Christ's death and resurrection:

Therefore we have been buried with Him through baptism into death, so that as Christ was raised from the dead through the glory of the Father, so we too might walk in newness of life. For if we have become united with Him in the likeness of His death, certainly we shall also be in the likeness of His resurrection.

Your submission to such teachings is critical to living like a champion today. By God's grace, through faith, believers become partakers in the divine nature and now share in the resurrection of Jesus Christ; in other words, we live in the victory of this future hope that allows us to persevere to the end and live with faith in the face of the most difficult of situations. Because we are partaking of His divine nature, our baptism is simultaneously a proclamation of our fellowship with the victory of God and of our escape from the corruption that is in the world.

Paul teaches in Ephesians 4:22-24, "In reference to your former manner of life, you lay aside the old self, which is being corrupted in accordance with the lusts of deceit, and that you be renewed in the spirit of your mind, and put on the new self, which in the likeness of God has been created in righteousness and holiness of the truth."

To learn how to live like a champion today, I need to define two terms from 2 Peter 1:3-4:

1) Promise. God has made specific commitments to His people through the covenants. There are specific precious and magnificent promises that we are to know! That is the point of the 40 Promises in 40 Days Challenge – to take time to examine specific promises of God and apply them to our lives, so that we can live like champions today.

2) Partakers of the divine nature. The best way to accurately understand this is to realize that the Greek word for "partaker" shares the same root word as *koinonia* which means, "fellowship." Partaking in the divine nature is not to *become* a god, but, rather, to have fellowship *with* God. Furthermore, it is to become God's partner in His divine power to bring about His precious and magnificent promises through Jesus, whom God sent because of His great love for the world (John 3:16).

We are called partners with God because of Christ's victory, not because of anything we bring to the table, but because of what God, in His love, has bestowed upon us. As Paul reminds us so clearly in his picture of this truth in 2 Corinthians 4:6-7:

> For God, who said, "Light shall shine out of darkness," is the One who has shone in our hearts to give the Light of the knowledge of the glory of God in the face of Christ. But we have this treasure in earthen vessels, so that the surpassing greatness of the power will be of God and not from ourselves.

Through His divine power, His precious and magnificent promises were "granted to us." According to the original language, this means that our status with God has been lavished upon us – bestowed by royalty. Its grammar (perfect participle) implies that this granting which was done in the past is still effective in the present and will continue to be so in the future. The promises are based on a past reality (justification) that will find fulfillment in the future (glorification) and is efficacious for today (sanctification).

John made this very clear in 1 John 3:1-3:

> See how great a love the Father has bestowed [lavished] on us, that we would be called children of God; and such we are. For this reason the world does not know us, because it did not know Him. Beloved, now we are children of God, and it has not appeared as yet what we will be. We know that when He appears, we will be like Him, because we will see Him just as He is. And everyone who has this hope fixed on Him purifies himself, just as He is pure.

We have a fellowship with God that will never end; it is eternal life, which begins at conversion through the indwelling of the Holy Spirit through faith in Jesus Christ. Then, progressively, our fellowship in the divine nature becomes more visible and effective as we grow in Christlikeness through the true knowledge of the Son of God and His precious and magnificent promises. This is God's divine work in each of us, and it is the zeal of the Lord of hosts which accomplishes this in and through us (Isaiah 9:7)!

Paul explained this in Philippians 1:6, 9-11:

For I am confident of this very thing, that He who began a good work in you will perfect it until the day of Christ Jesus. ... And this I pray, that your love may abound still more and more in real knowledge and all discernment, so that you may approve the things that are excellent, in order to be sincere and blameless until the day of Christ; having been filled with the fruit of righteousness which comes through Jesus Christ, to the glory and praise of God.

Thomas Schreiner in *The New American Commentary* explained:

God has given saving promises to his people, so that they will become like God. They will become like God and are becoming like God because they have escaped "the corruption in the world caused by evil desires." Once again, some scholars argue that believers will escape the corruption of the world at death or when the Lord returns. It is more likely, however, that Peter operated with an already-but-not-yet schema. Believers have already escaped the world's corruption in that they belong to God, but the full realization of such a liberation will be theirs on the day of resurrection.[6]

This is the ethical reality of partaking in the divine nature. This is the praxis of the promise! Every promise of God comes with choices regarding how we are to live: the commissions and omissions of God's promises!

Paul was very clear in 1 Corinthians 10:20-21 that, once we belong to Christ, we are to break fellowship with this world and that which has caused its corruption through lust: "but I say that the things which the Gentiles sacrifice, they sacrifice to demons and not to God; and I do not want you to become sharers in demons. You cannot drink the cup of the Lord and the cup of demons; you cannot partake of the table of the Lord and the table of demons."

We are no longer to have fellowship with the corruption of this world caused by lust. That is our holy omission within the Great Commission! The key to this reality is that every "no" you say to your lusts is so that you can experience the better "yes" of partaking in God's blessings in your everyday life.

The promise that we will partake of the divine nature is not exclusively the gospel proclamation that we will not perish but have everlasting life with God in Heaven. Through the resurrection of Jesus Christ, we have not only escaped the mortality of this perishable body (1 Corinthians 15), but we are also taking on the life of Jesus Christ. That is, the sharing in the moral qualities of who Jesus Christ is, and joining Him in His mission on Earth; this is why He came and the purpose for our rescue. When you share the nature of something or someone, you take on their qualities and character. You become the fruit of that to which you are grafted. You are a branch upon the vine that bears His fruit (John 15).

---

6 Thomas R. Schreiner, *1, 2 Peter, Jude*, vol. 37, The New American Commentary (Nashville: Broadman & Holman Publishers, 2003), 293–296.

Peter taught us that we have everything we need, through His divine power, for godliness and life. That's a promise about the precious and magnificent promises that have been lavished upon us through the victory of Jesus Christ. "It is done" is both the promise of resurrection (John 19:30) and of consummation (Revelation 21:6), both of which are guaranteed to us through Jesus Christ.

The promises of God equip us with everything we need to live like a champion today. They are a both-and, for this life and the next, for salvation and sanctification, for Heaven and Earth!

The promises of God give us the hope to keep the faith, and the faith to love, and the love to be like Jesus – to live like a champion today!

Here is an illustration using a common phrase from Christianity: What would you think if I were to say to you, or one of your loved ones, "May you rest in peace"? Most likely, it would be heard as a harbinger of death and not appreciated by you or anyone in the family.

Honestly though, if we understood the promises of God, we should pray this for one another every night, and every Sabbath day, and even, if we are willing to learn how to be a yokefellow of Jesus, as we work hard in our day-to-day lives.

The rest that God promises is not just for heaven, but also for this life! I could make a convincing argument that the greatest evangelistic witness we could display right now in our frenetic "25/8" culture is to be peaceful and restful, from the inside out.

Jesus promises in Matthew 11:28-30, "Come to Me, all who are weary and heavy-laden, and I will give you rest. Take My yoke upon you and learn from Me, for I am gentle and humble in heart, and you will find rest for your souls. For My yoke is easy and My burden is light."

Every precious and magnificent promise of Jesus comes with a praxis – it's found in His yoke! The yoke is an agricultural metaphor for coming into the Christian life of discipleship, the life of obedience and submission to God, under the power of the Spirit. We experience peace by learning to live in the yoke of Jesus.

Let me connect the yokefellow concept of Matthew 11:28-30 back to 2 Peter 1. Richard Bauckham explained in the Word Biblical Commentary about 2 Peter 1:3:

> By the divine power evident in Christ's life, death and resurrection he has called men and women to be Christians, and when they come to knowledge of Christ in Christian conversion they also receive through that knowledge the grace of Christ which will enable them to live a life of obedience to God.[7]

Furthermore, this is your partaking of the divine nature – your "fellowship with the Spirit" as Paul invited us to in Philippians 2:1-2, "Therefore if there is any encouragement in Christ, if there is any consolation of love, if there is any fellowship of the Spirit, if any affection and compassion, make my joy complete by being of the same mind, maintaining the same love, united in spirit, intent on one purpose" (cf. 2 Corinthians 13:14).

In other words, outside of the yoke of Jesus there is no peace because outside of His yoke there is no relationship with God ... so, rest in peace! In our fellowship with God, we are partaking of Him and His nature; we are learning to walk as He walked, in the power of the Holy Spirit (1 John 2:6).

To complete this illustration: "Rest in peace" is a promise with a praxis, yes for Heaven, but more so for today, just as Paul promised in Philippians

---

7 Richard J. Bauckham, *2 Peter, Jude*, vol. 50, Word Biblical Commentary (Dallas: Word, Incorporated, 1983), 192–193.

4:7, 9: "And the peace of God, which surpasses all comprehension, will guard your hearts and your minds in Christ Jesus. … The things you have learned and received and heard and seen in me, practice these things, and the God of peace will be with you."

The promises of God teach us how to live faithfully on a day-to-day basis. This is the content of the promises of Jesus Christ – the same divine power that gives us hope of eternal life directs and empowers how we live today when we choose to partake in His divine nature.

In fact, that is the exact intent of Peter who bookends his letter with this reality in 2 Peter 3:13-18, the last verse of Peter's letter:

> But according to His promise we are looking for new heavens and a new earth, in which righteousness dwells. Therefore, beloved, since you look for these things, be diligent to be found by Him in peace, spotless and blameless, and regard the patience of our Lord as salvation; just as also our beloved brother Paul, according to the wisdom given him, wrote to you, as also in all his letters, speaking in them of these things, in which are some things hard to understand, which the untaught and unstable distort, as they do also the rest of the Scriptures, to their own destruction. You, therefore, beloved, knowing this beforehand, be on your guard so that you are not carried away by the error of unprincipled men and fall from your own steadfastness, but grow in the grace and knowledge of our Lord and Savior Jesus Christ. To Him be the glory, both now and to the day of eternity. Amen.

The precious and magnificent promises of God are a both-and! They are your future hope and your present faith! God is inviting you to have fellowship with Him through His Son Jesus Christ. In fellowship with Him, every promise of God is yours because He is yours – you are partaking in

His divine nature! You are living like a champion today because you are living in partnership with the Champion.

Chapter 4
The Promise of Effectiveness and Fruitfulness

Now for this very reason also, applying all diligence, in your faith
supply moral excellence, and in your moral excellence, knowledge,
and in your knowledge, self-control, and in your self-control,
perseverance, and in your perseverance, godliness, and in your
godliness, brotherly kindness, and in your brotherly kindness, love.
For if these qualities are yours and are increasing, they render you
neither useless nor unfruitful in the true knowledge of our Lord Jesus
Christ. For he who lacks these qualities is blind or short-sighted,
having forgotten his purification from his former sins.
2 Peter 1:5-9

The opening clause "Now for this very reason" is referencing the reality of
2 Peter 1:4, "For by these He has granted to us His precious and
magnificent promises, so that by them you may become partakers of the
divine nature, having escaped the corruption that is in the world by lust."

As we learned in the previous chapter, to be a "partaker of the divine
nature" is to be in fellowship with God. It is to be in union with Jesus
Christ through the fellowship of the Holy Spirit. This is God's sovereign
will for our lives, as stated by Paul in Romans 8:29-30:

> For those whom He foreknew, He also predestined to become
> conformed to the image of His Son, so that He would be the firstborn
> among many brethren; and these whom He predestined, He also called;
> and these whom He called, He also justified; and these whom He
> justified, He also glorified.

This is a triple blessing – past justification, future glorification, and our
present godliness (or progressive sanctification), which is the intent of this

passage and to which we are to apply all diligence.

The opening clause continues, "Now for this very reason also, applying all diligence …" We are invited to participate in God's divine nature through our diligence! This is the truth of Philippians 2:12b-13, "Work out your salvation with fear and trembling; [Yes, we are to apply all diligence to our godliness, but listen to verse 13] for it is God who is at work in you, both to will and to work for His good pleasure."

To be very clear, again, our fellowship in God's divine nature is a promise to take on God's characteristics through our union with Jesus and fellowship with His Spirit. It is not a promise to become a god; rather, it's a call to share in the eternal life of God (His immortality), as well as in His mission on Earth by partnering with God and taking on the character and life of Jesus (His morality).

Just as the author of Hebrews exhorts all believers in Hebrews 3:14, "For we have become partakers of Christ, if we hold fast the beginning of our assurance firm until the end." This is the invitation of God's grace!

We are to be diligent in living our eternal life today by partaking in His divine nature. We are called to manifest the new morality of Jesus, in increasing measure (progressively more!), as we remember our past justification and our future glorification. These are done; the victory is ours in Christ – now live like it! Live like a champion today!

In the words of Jesus from John 15, we are to bear His fruit because we are branches connected to Him, the vine; we are demonstrating to the world by manifesting good fruit in this life that we truly are sharing in His divine nature. You will know the partners of God by their fruit – God's trees are effective and fruitful!

That is what Peter is explaining in 2 Peter 1:8-9, "For if these qualities are yours and are increasing [abounding], they render you neither useless nor unfruitful in the true knowledge of our Lord Jesus Christ. For he who lacks these qualities is blind or short-sighted, having forgotten his purification from his former sins."

Do you want to be effective and fruitful in living as a partner with God through Christ's victory?

Here's the key – preach the gospel of Jesus to yourself every single day! Never forget that, though you were once hell-bent, you are now heaven-bound! You were once dead in sin; you are now alive in Christ!

We are invited to apply 2 Peter 1:5-7 as a praxis of our everyday lives so that we can learn how to live like a champion today:

> Now for this very reason also, applying all diligence, in your faith supply moral excellence, and in your moral excellence, knowledge, and in your knowledge, self-control, and in your self-control, perseverance, and in your perseverance, godliness, and in your godliness, brotherly kindness, and in your brotherly kindness, love.

This diligence is our Christian discipleship, and the heart of all discipleship is the work of the Holy Spirit to transform us through the renewing of our minds into Christlikeness, which is our sharing in His nature. Paul taught us this about spiritual formation in Romans 12:1-2:

> Therefore I urge you, brethren, by the mercies of God, to present your bodies a living and holy sacrifice, acceptable to God, which is your spiritual service of worship. And do not be conformed to this world, but be transformed by the renewing of your mind, so that you may prove what the will of God is, that which is good and acceptable and perfect.

According to God's Word from 2 Peter 1:5-7, we are to be diligent in the process of spiritual formation in the following sequential way:

1) Faith supplies moral excellence. Faith is the preexisting condition! Morality is an outflow (a product or fruit) of God's good gift of faith to you. Moralism, the enemy of Christ, is when you strive in the flesh for what only God can produce in the Spirit!

Paul very clearly said in Romans 12:3, "For through the grace given to me I say to everyone among you not to think more highly of himself than he ought to think; but to think so as to have sound judgment, as God has allotted to each a measure of faith."

Faith is what supplies moral excellence; therefore, no trust can be put in the flesh for one's spiritual formation. Galatians 3:3 further teaches us the significance of the Spirit and not the flesh: "Are you so foolish? Having begun by the Spirit, are you now being perfected by the flesh?"

2) Moral excellence increases knowledge. Moral excellence is the other side of the coin of partaking of the divine nature. As Christ welcomed us in the eternal life of the Father, He could only do that by first removing our sin; this is our escape of the corruption that is in the world by lust (2 Peter 1:4).

As moral excellence increases, so does our hunger and thirst for the true knowledge of God in Jesus Christ. Paul emphasized in Philippians 3:8, "More than that, I count all things to be loss in view of the surpassing value of knowing Christ Jesus my Lord, for whom I have suffered the loss of all things, and count them but rubbish so that I may gain Christ."

3) Knowing Christ Jesus leads to self-control. Self-control is the last of the fruit of the Spirit (Galatians 5:22-23). As Paul said to Timothy in 2

Timothy 1:7, "For God has not given us a spirit of timidity, but of power and love and discipline [sound mind]." Love and self-control are the effective bookends of a champion's life.

4) Self-control grows perseverance. There is nothing our bodies want more than a stress-free, pain-free, pleasurable experience. It is our faith which deeply roots us in Christ through the storms of life. As James 1:12 explains, "Blessed is a man who perseveres under trial; for once he has been approved, he will receive the crown of life which the Lord has promised to those who love Him."

5) Perseverance is what trains us in godliness. We must never bail before the blessing of Christlikeness, because God uses all things in our lives to conform us into the image of Christ Jesus. This is the "called according to His purpose" of Romans 8:28-30 that allows us to persevere through suffering and hardship.

Paul explains in Romans 5:3-5, "We also exult in our tribulations, knowing that tribulation brings about perseverance; and perseverance, proven character; and proven character, hope; and hope does not disappoint, because the love of God has been poured out within our hearts through the Holy Spirit who was given to us."

6) Godliness manifests in brotherly kindness (*philadelphia*). The truth of your fellowship with God is found in your fellowship with others. John unapologetically taught us this in 1 John 3:14-18:

We know that we have passed out of death into life, because we love the brethren. He who does not love abides in death. Everyone who hates his brother is a murderer; and you know that no murderer has eternal life abiding in him. We know love by this, that He laid down His life for us; and we ought to lay down our lives for the brethren. But whoever has the world's goods, and sees his brother in need and closes his heart against him, how does the love of God abide in him? Little children, let us not love with word or with tongue, but in deed and truth.

7) Brotherly kindness expresses God's love (*agape*). God's love is the example of Jesus Christ, who is the fullness of God dwelling in flesh (Colossians 1:19). Jesus is our example for what it truly looks like to escape the corruption of the world and become a partaker of the divine nature.

Jesus' words are very clear in John 13:34-35, "A new commandment I give to you, that you love one another, even as I have loved you, that you also love one another. By this all men will know that you are My disciples, if you have love for one another."

This is our way to effectiveness and fruitfulness! This is our training regimen so that we can grow up in Christlikeness and embody His love and grace to the world. We are each chosen and called members of the same team. For us to be effective and fruitful, we each must be diligent in our training in godliness, so that as we, God's team, hear the Coach's voice, we can run the right play at the right time, according to His playbook, as the many unique members of His one unified body (Romans 12:4-5). Live like a champion today!

Chapter 5
The Promise of Eternity Fuels the Life of a Champion

Therefore, brethren, be all the more diligent to make certain about
His calling and choosing you; for as long as you practice these
things, you will never stumble; for in this way the entrance into the
eternal kingdom of our Lord and Savior Jesus Christ will be
abundantly supplied to you.
2 Peter 1:10-11

If you had confidence that the championship was secure, then you would memorize the playbook, train with confidence, trust and listen to your coach, and work together with the other players on the team. You would play like a champion today!

In Christ, we have the promise of eternity. It is done! This is the overarching truth for living a victorious life because this is the foundation of all our faith, hope, and love.

The athletes of God must cultivate hope in Jesus so that we may live by faith and not by sight, as Paul commands us in 2 Corinthians 5:1-10:

For we know that if the earthly tent which is our house is torn down, we have a building from God, a house not made with hands, eternal in the heavens. For indeed in this house we groan, longing to be clothed with our dwelling from heaven, inasmuch as we, having put it on, will not be found naked. For indeed while we are in this tent, we groan, being burdened, because we do not want to be unclothed but to be clothed, so that what is mortal will be swallowed up by life. Now He who prepared us for this very purpose is God, who gave to us the Spirit as a pledge. Therefore, being always of good courage, and knowing that while we are at home in the body we are absent from the Lord - for we walk by faith, not by sight - we are of good courage, I say, and prefer rather to be absent from the body and to be at home with the Lord. Therefore we also have as our ambition, whether at home or absent, to be pleasing to Him. For we must all appear before the judgment seat of Christ, so that each one may be recompensed for his deeds in the body, according to what he has done, whether good or bad.

How then shall we live? As we examine 2 Peter 1:10-11, we observe the progression of Peter's thinking.

We, the "brethren," the members of Christ's body, are to "be all the more diligent to make certain about His calling and choosing." This is in the imperative form meaning it is a command from the Coach to each athlete on His team – be diligent to not forget "[your] purification from [your] former sins" (2 Peter 1:9)!

Remember your calling! As an athlete on the winning team, you need to be diligent in knowing that you have been called to the team by the Coach because He chose you. The original language is saying, "to make this a permanent experience" or to be diligent in "securing" this truth in you. You made the cut, you're on the roster, and you are getting playing time because the Coach chose you, believes in you, and is putting you on the field.

Jesus has unapologetically told you this truth in John 15:16, "You did not choose Me but I chose you, and appointed you that you would go and bear fruit, and that your fruit would remain, so that whatever you ask of the Father in My name He may give to you."

You have been handpicked to be a part of God's team! How can you be "all the more diligent" to know this?

Your diligence is evidenced through your effectiveness and fruitfulness "in the true knowledge of our Lord Jesus Christ" (2 Peter 1:8). It is through fruit-bearing that we are certain of God's choosing. As Jesus said in John

15:8, "My Father is glorified by this, that you bear much fruit, and so prove to be My disciples" (cf. Ephesians 2:8-10).

As a "partaker of the divine nature," you are sharing in His nature, a partner of God in His purposes and plans. Jesus spoke this to an agricultural community not only in those words of being a fruit-bearing branch abiding in the vine, but also in the words of being fruit-bearing trees in Matthew 12:33-37:

Either make the tree good and its fruit good, or make the tree bad and its fruit bad; for the tree is known by its fruit. You brood of vipers, how can you, being evil, speak what is good? For the mouth speaks out of that which fills the heart. The good man brings out of his good treasure what is good; and the evil man brings out of his evil treasure what is evil. But I tell you that every careless word that people speak, they shall give an accounting for it in the day of judgment. For by your words you will be justified, and by your words you will be condemned.

You produce (manifest and so prove to be) according to your kind. As Peter states in 2 Peter 1:4, if you are sharing in the divine nature of God, then you have escaped the corruption of this world (cf. Romans 12:1-2).

Earlier, in John 8:31-32, Jesus made it very clear what that meant to those who believed in Him, "If you continue in My word, then you are truly disciples of Mine; and you will know the truth, and the truth will make you free."

Did you hear that? His abiding truth will make you free! Jesus rescued you so that you can live in His victory every day of your life. Living like a champion is a way of life – it is living eternally today!

There is something very beautiful in the original language of 2 Peter 1:10: "Therefore, brethren, be all the more diligent to make certain about

His calling and choosing you; for as long as you practice these things, you will never stumble." The verb "to make" is in the middle voice. Listen to this quote from a Greek Grammar book, "the middle voice signifies that the subject performs the action of the verb <u>and</u> participates somehow in the results."[8] You both perform the action of making certain, and participate in the certainty, of God's action to secure you as His own. Jesus has rescued you <u>and</u> you have escaped! Learning to live like a champion today is a call to live in the middle voice of God's choosing you to be a member of His championship team! **It is done, now do it!**

As Peter says in 2 Peter 1:10, "for as long as you practice these things [the virtues of 2 Peter 1:5-7], you will never stumble." The promises of God come with praxes – daily invitations to practice what you believe, putting into practice the faith you have received. You are saved by faith alone, absolutely, but faith never stands alone! You are known by the works of your faith, as James stated in James 1:22-25:

> But prove yourselves doers of the word, and not merely hearers who delude themselves. For if anyone is a hearer of the word and not a doer, he is like a man who looks at his natural face in a mirror; for once he has looked at himself and gone away, he has immediately forgotten what kind of person he was. But one who looks intently at the perfect law, the law of liberty, and abides by it, not having become a forgetful hearer but an effectual doer, this man will be blessed in what he does.

The logic of Scripture is irrefutable, as James' words harken us back to when Peter said in 2 Peter 1:8-9, "For if these qualities are yours and are

---

8 Fredrick J. Long, *Kairos: A Beginning Greek Grammar* (Mishawaka, IN: Fredrick J. Long, 2005), 28. Underline added.

increasing, they render you neither useless nor unfruitful in the true knowledge of our Lord Jesus Christ. For he who lacks these qualities is blind or short-sighted, having forgotten his purification from his former sins."

We are to build our lives on the words of Jesus. We are to practice "these things" so that we will never stumble. This is the promise of Jesus Christ as the benediction of Jude 24-25 proclaims the power of God through Jesus Christ: "Now to Him who is able to keep you from stumbling, and to make you stand in the presence of His glory blameless with great joy, to the only God our Savior, through Jesus Christ our Lord, be glory, majesty, dominion and authority, before all time and now and forever. Amen."

John says something strikingly similar in 1 John 3:1-3:

See how great a love the Father has bestowed on us, that we would be called children of God; and such we are. For this reason the world does not know us, because it did not know Him. Beloved, now we are children of God, and it has not appeared as yet what we will be. We know that when He appears, we will be like Him, because we will see Him just as He is. And everyone who has this hope fixed on Him purifies himself, just as He is pure.

Both Scriptures bring us back to Peter's logic in 2 Peter 1:11, "for in this way the entrance into the eternal kingdom of our Lord and Savior Jesus Christ will be abundantly supplied to you."

I love the visual of this promise regarding eternal life: the entrance into the eternal kingdom will be abundantly supplied to you. How is that possible?

Jesus taught us very clearly about the entrance (or gate) to life in

Matthew 7:13-14, "Enter through the narrow gate; for the gate is wide and the way is broad that leads to destruction, and there are many who enter through it. For the gate is small and the way is narrow that leads to life, and there are few who find it."

How is the entrance abundantly supplied, yet the gate small, and the way narrow?

These two truths are brought into perfect unity through the exclusive means of Jesus Christ; as He said in John 14:6, "I am the way, and the truth, and the life; no one comes to the Father but through Me."

The hope of entering the eternal dominion and authority of our Lord and Savior Jesus Christ is abundantly supplied to us through a personal relationship with Him. It is in Christ alone! Jesus is the most inclusively exclusive entry point into eternal life. Jesus gives us His abundant life with the Father! Apart from Him, there is no entry way – He is the only mediator of the covenant between God and humanity (1 Timothy 2:5).

Jesus Christ returned to agricultural imagery to make this point very clear in John 10:1-10:

> Truly, truly, I say to you, he who does not enter by the door into the fold of the sheep, but climbs up some other way, he is a thief and a robber. But he who enters by the door is a shepherd of the sheep. To him the doorkeeper opens, and the sheep hear his voice, and he calls his own sheep by name and leads them out. When he puts forth all his own, he goes ahead of them, and the sheep follow him because they know his voice. A stranger they simply will not follow, but will flee from him, because they do not know the voice of strangers. This figure of speech Jesus spoke to them, but they did not understand what those things were which He had been saying to them. So Jesus said to them again, Truly, truly, I say to you, I am the door of the sheep. All who

came before Me are thieves and robbers, but the sheep did not hear them. I am the door; if anyone enters through Me, he will be saved, and will go in and out and find pasture. The thief comes only to steal and kill and destroy; I came that they may have life, and have it abundantly.

When you live in this abundance of eternal life, you face each day with hope and that hope will cause you never to lose faith. Faith and hope work within you to empower the love of God to manifest through you in every circumstance you face. When you face your days with faith, hope, and love, then there is no circumstance that you cannot overcome because God is with you and His victory belongs to you in Christ Jesus. Therefore, brethren, go and diligently practice the fruit of your eternal life, today: "love, joy, peace, patience, kindness, goodness, faithfulness, gentleness, [and] self-control" (Galatians 5:22-23). This is your eternal life manifesting to the world that you belong to God and are partaking of His divine power.

This is living like a champion today! It is living with the character of Jesus Christ, which is only possible through the indwelling power of God in you. It is the Holy Spirit who fuels the lives of His champions!

Chapter 6
The Promise of a Trustworthy Playbook

Therefore, I will always be ready to remind you of these things, even though you already know them, and have been established in the truth which is present with you. I consider it right, as long as I am in this earthly dwelling, to stir you up by way of reminder, knowing that the laying aside of my earthly dwelling is imminent, as also our Lord Jesus Christ has made clear to me. And I will also be diligent that at any time after my departure you will be able to call these things to mind. For we did not follow cleverly devised tales when we made known to you the power and coming of our Lord Jesus Christ, but we were eyewitnesses of His majesty. For when He received honor and glory from God the Father, such an utterance as this was made to Him by the Majestic Glory, "This is My beloved Son with whom I am well-pleased" – and we ourselves heard this utterance made from heaven when we were with Him on the holy mountain. So we have the prophetic word made more sure, to which you do well to pay attention as to a lamp shining in a dark place, until the day dawns and the morning star arises in your hearts. But know this first of all, that no prophecy of Scripture is a matter of one's own interpretation, for no prophecy was ever made by an act of human will, but men moved by the Holy Spirit spoke from God.
2 Peter 1:12-21

Champions trust that the Bible is God's Word – a trustworthy playbook to win the victory in their everyday lives.

As of first importance, 2 Peter 1:20-21 speaks of the inspiration of God's Word: "But know this first of all, that no prophecy of Scripture is a matter of one's own interpretation, for no prophecy was ever made by an act of human will, but men moved by the Holy Spirit spoke from God."

The Bible is God-breathed (inspired), as Paul teaches in 2 Timothy 3:16-17, "All Scripture is inspired by God and profitable for teaching, for reproof, for correction, for training in righteousness; so that the man of God may be adequate, equipped for every good work."

Furthermore, the four Gospel narratives are the true historical accounts of Jesus Christ, the living Word. Peter, a disciple of Jesus, makes significant claims of his first-hand witness to their historicity in 2 Peter 1:16-18:

> For we did not follow cleverly devised tales when we made known to you the power and coming of our Lord Jesus Christ, but we were eyewitnesses of His majesty. For when He received honor and glory from God the Father, such an utterance as this was made to Him by the Majestic Glory, "This is My beloved Son with whom I am well-pleased – and we ourselves heard this utterance made from heaven when we were with Him on the holy mountain.

Luke further emphasizes the accuracy of the Gospels as theologically motivated historical accounts of Jesus' life and ministry in Luke 1:1-4, the prelude of his Gospel:

> Inasmuch as many have undertaken to compile an account of the things accomplished among us, just as they were handed down to us by those who from the beginning were eyewitnesses and servants of the word, it seemed fitting for me as well, having investigated everything carefully from the beginning, to write it out for you in consecutive order, most excellent Theophilus; so that you may know the exact truth about the things you have been taught.

As a final point of the importance of the Word of God, Peter states in 2 Peter 1:19, "So we have the prophetic word made more sure, to which you do well to pay attention as to a lamp shining in a dark place, until the day dawns and the morning star arises in your hearts."

John, another first-hand witness of Jesus, discussed Jesus with the same imagery in John 1:1-4:

In the beginning was the Word, and the Word was with God, and the Word was God. He was in the beginning with God. All things came into being through Him, and apart from Him nothing came into being that has come into being. In Him was life, and the life was the Light of men. The Light shines in the darkness, and the darkness did not comprehend it.

If the first big step of living like a champion today is to know God's playbook, then God's players must hold to the conviction that, as we learn to listen to God's voice, we will trust the Bible as His playbook. When God calls us into the game and directs us to play a certain play, we won't question the authenticity (that this is the Coach's idea and not our own) or the efficacy of that play (that the play will accomplish that which the Coach intends for it to do).

We are invited to trust the Bible as God's playbook. The Coach teaches us this in Isaiah 55:10-11:

For as the rain and the snow come down from heaven, and do not return there without watering the earth and making it bear and sprout, and furnishing seed to the sower and bread to the eater; so will My word be which goes forth from My mouth; it will not return to Me empty, without accomplishing what I desire, and without succeeding in the matter for which I sent it.

Can you imagine the ridiculously chaotic game on the football field if the players started questioning the authenticity or efficacy of the play every huddle? There would be no game. There would be only internal confusion and fighting at every huddle (with no running of the plays; therefore, no victory!).

Is this an accurate image for the American church? We spend more time in our huddles "discussing" the authenticity and trustworthiness of the playbook and questioning the efficacy of the plays themselves, and we never get on with the game to win the championship!

You can change that in your local church by applying what you have learned from the 40 Promises in 40 Days Challenge. Every day for the rest of your life, you can live like a champion today by following the four action steps of this book with every word from God's Word:

1) Know God's playbook.
2) Train for Godliness.
3) Listen to the Coach.
4) Work together with God's team.

These four action steps are not only the key to learning to live like a champion today, they are an effective way to read God's Word and apply it to your life. Whether you use a trusted devotional book like my *Seize the Moment* devotional series, or you read through the Bible yourself one verse, or one chapter, per day, you can approach God's Word like a champion by applying the four actions steps of this book to it. When you invite others to do this with you, then you start calling forth God's championship team in your local community. There is no telling what God will do when a small group of committed champions starts living their lives according to God's game plan in fellowship with other teammates. Pray about who God would have you invite to join you in bringing the victory to your community. It starts with you – live like a champion today!

We are to build our lives and our game plan on the truth of God's Word, straight from the playbook, play by play, verse by verse, and chapter by chapter! God has given us His Word and His Spirit to do what Peter promises in 2 Peter 1:12-15:

> Therefore, I will always be ready to remind you of these things, even though you already know them, and have been established in the truth which is present with you. I consider it right, as long as I am in this earthly dwelling, to stir you up by way of reminder, knowing that the laying aside of my earthly dwelling is imminent, as also our Lord Jesus Christ has made clear to me. And I will also be diligent that at any time after my departure you will be able to call these things to mind.

Let's review how that happens so that you can take the good fruit of this book and the 40-Day Challenge into the rest of your life:

1) His Word is the playbook! We establish our lives on the truth of God's Word as handed down to us in the Bible.

We do this by memorizing and internalizing God's Word as individual players. Psalm 119:9-12 teaches us how we, the athletes on God's team, should approach His playbook for our lives:

> How can a young man keep his way pure? By keeping it according to Your word. With all my heart I have sought You; Do not let me wander from Your commandments. Your word I have treasured in my

heart, That I may not sin against You. Blessed are You, O LORD; Teach me Your statutes.

2) His Church is God's Team! We come together to encourage one another and be reminded that, as a team, we are called to run the plays in the Bible together. As Hebrews 10:23-25 commands each of us as players on the same team:

> Let us hold fast the confession of our hope without wavering, for He who promised is faithful; and let us consider how to stimulate one another to love and good deeds, not forsaking our own assembling together, as is the habit of some, but encouraging one another; and all the more as you see the day drawing near.

Living like a champion today is intended to be learned and practiced together, but must be experienced every day outside the four walls of a local church. The huddles and the practices are necessary, but the Christian life was never meant to be one big holy huddle; rather, every local church is intended to have a rhythm of gathering and scattering, so that we run the right play in the everyday circumstances and challenges of our communities. This is how we live on mission for the glory of God!

3) The Holy Spirit speaks the Coach's voice to us! The Holy Spirit is the one who stirs us up and calls the play for the Coach during our ever-present circumstances and challenges. God has given us the Word, and He calls us to the right play from the Word through the Spirit!

Jesus promised us this in John 14:26, "But the Helper, the Holy Spirit, whom the Father will send in My name, He will teach you all things, and bring to your remembrance all that I said to you" (cf. Luke 12:11-12).

4) Seize the moment and make His victory visible daily! As we learn the playbook and listen to our Coach's voice, then we can seize the moment and live like champions in both the public and private arenas of our lives, making His victory visible every day. This is our great evangelistic witness to our communities and the nations. We are to shine God's victorious light everywhere we go (Matthew 5:14-16). Paul teaches us in Philippians 2:12-16:

> So then, my beloved, just as you have always obeyed, not as in my presence only, but now much more in my absence, work out your salvation with fear and trembling; for it is God who is at work in you, both to will and to work for His good pleasure. Do all things without grumbling or disputing; so that you will prove yourselves to be blameless and innocent, children of God above reproach in the midst of a crooked and perverse generation, among whom you appear as lights in the world, holding fast the word of life, so that in the day of Christ I will have reason to glory because I did not run in vain nor toil in vain (cf. Matthew 5:14-16 & 1 Peter 2:9-12).

Ultimately, as athletes on God's team, we live like champions today so that others will come to know the One who gave us His Victory!

CONCLUSION

My sixth and final throw in the 2000 USA Track & Field Olympic Team Trials was a clutch throw at the biggest competition of my life; it was my best effort of the day and my best performance on the biggest national stage for any track and field athlete. I had done it! I had performed under pressure, but so did Jud Logan. Jud earned his fourth Olympic Team berth in his final throw and, heartbreakingly, moved me from being on the Olympic Team to sitting in an alternate spot, which meant little to nothing as a hammer thrower. I had devoted myself, worked through injuries, and made sacrifices to make the team, but Jud was better than me on that day. I am proud of him for doing his best, and I have nothing to be ashamed of from my life of devotion, but I fell short of the goal to which I had committed my life.

After narrowly missing the Olympic Team in 2000, I was crushed! I had devoted a significant amount of time and energy in the most vital years of my early career in the US Army to make it to the biggest stage in sport. I worked hard and pushed myself to the max. I dealt with the adversities of being an active-duty officer expected to serve in difficult duties and maintain my military preparedness while training my body to do something that was not aligned with those military standards. I fought through injuries and sickness to do my very best. I resumed training for the Olympics after attending the Infantry Officer Basic Course and Ranger School, and after serving as a Platoon Leader in the 82nd Airborne Division. I was pushing myself – heart, mind, body, and soul to be the very best I could be in every area of my life.

I had accepted the challenge! Little did I know at the time, or for many years, that I was pushing myself too hard and overtraining athletically, plus pushing my mind, heart, and body to their breaking points. I was devoted, but I was paying a steep price! While the US Army's World Class Athlete Program rewarded me and brought me to the Pentagon to be showcased as a successful soldier-athlete, I felt like a failure! While USA Track & Field applauded my efforts, and later invited me to be an athlete representative to their board of directors, I felt like a fraud! I was growing hollow on the inside.

It took me years of reflection to realize that I had accepted the wrong challenge. I was a passionate and dedicated young man; whether it was my work as a soldier, athlete, or student, I had excelled by devoting myself to the task. But the tasks left me empty and incomplete because they could never fulfill the deepest need of my soul. There was a call, higher and greater, inviting me to become more than I could ever imagine being. When I finally got it, I left everything behind to accept the call of Jesus upon my life to follow Him. I have never regretted accepting this greatest challenge, bestowed by my loving Father, to me, through His Son.

I don't know what dreams have a grip on your heart or mind. I don't know what you push yourself for, or what weight is crushing you, but please know there is One who has made a way for you to live like a champion today. Jesus Christ invites you in Matthew 11:28-30, "Come to Me, all who are weary and heavy-laden, and I will give you rest. Take My yoke upon you and learn from Me, for I am gentle and humble in heart, and you will find rest for your souls. For My yoke is easy and My burden is light."

The purpose of this book has been to help you accept the right challenge – the challenge of learning how to live like a champion today! I have chased dreams across the country and to some amazing places overseas, only to find myself crushed under the weight of those dreams. The good news is that God sent His Son Jesus Christ from Heaven to Earth to win you (and me!) over to God's team where you are already a champion in Him! This is what Christ has done for you, and this is what this book has offered you to find out and experience for yourself. You must decide what you will do with His gracious invitation.

Will you take onto yourself a personal relationship with Jesus Christ by giving Him the burden of your sin and the weariness of your soul? Will you put your faith in Jesus Christ today and ask Him to forgive you of your sin? Will you confess Him as the Son of God who died on the Cross and defeated death, rising from the grave after three days? Will you commit the rest of your life to have Him as your Lord and Savior, learning to obey His Word, becoming like Him from the inside out through the power of God's Spirit who dwells in you? Will you trust God with every area of your life today?

The challenge, now that you've completed the 40 Promises in 40 Days Challenge, is to accept Jesus' invitation, live in His easy yoke, and learn from Him to find rest for your soul. This is the journey of learning to trust God to keep His promises every time and in every way. While the journey is long and challenging, it always starts with a step and continues one step at a time. The fulfillment of this challenge is that you, like Jesus, will become gentle and humble in heart, meaning that you will be submissive to the Father's will for your life, walking closely with Him to experience His victory as you face the difficulties of the day.

Believe God for His great and magnificent promises; the victorious life of Jesus Christ is the life of faith! As John says in 1 John 5:4b, "This is the victory that has overcome the world – our faith." Jesus Christ is the Champion of your soul. In light of the ultimate victory of THE Champion, live like a champion today!

APPENDIX

THE 40 PROMISES IN 40 DAYS CHALLENGE MEMORY CARDS

Cards can also be downloaded at
https://agfpublishingcompany.com/the-40-promises-in-40-days-challenge-memory-cards/

Day 1: The Promise of Grace

2 Corinthians 12:9 (NAS95)

"And [Jesus] has said to me, 'My grace is sufficient for you, for power is perfected in weakness.' Most gladly, therefore, I will rather boast about my weaknesses, so that the power of Christ may dwell in me."

Day 2: The Promise of Resurrection and Life

John 11:25-26 (NAS95)

"Jesus said to her, 'I am the resurrection and the life; he who believes in Me will live even if he dies, and everyone who lives and believes in Me will never die. Do you believe this?'"

Day 3: The Promise of the Holy Spirit

John 14:26 (NAS95)

"But the Helper, the Holy Spirit, whom the Father will send in My name, He will teach you all things, and bring to your remembrance all that I said to you."

Day 4: The Promise of Gathering

Hebrews 10:24-25 (NAS95)

"Let us consider how to stimulate one another to love and good deeds, not forsaking our own assembling together, as is the habit of some, but encouraging one another; and all the more as you see the day drawing near."

Day 5: The Promise of Security

Romans 8:38-39 (NAS95)

"For I am convinced that neither death, nor life, nor angels, nor principalities, nor things present, nor things to come, nor powers, nor height, nor depth, nor any other created thing, will be able to separate us from the love of God, which is in Christ Jesus our Lord."

Day 6: The Promise of a New Beginning

2 Corinthians 5:17 (NAS95)

"Therefore if anyone is in Christ, he is a new creature; the old things passed away; behold, new things have come."

Day 7: The Promise of Faith

Romans 12:3 (NAS95)

"For through the grace given to me I say to everyone among you not to think more highly of himself than he ought to think; but to think so as to have sound judgment, as God has allotted to each a measure of faith."

Day 8: The Promise of Membership

Romans 12:4-5 (NAS95)

"For just as we have many members in one body and all the members do not have the same function, so we, who are many, are one body in Christ, and individually members one of another."

Day 9: The Promise of Adoption

Romans 8:15 (NAS95)

"For you have not received a spirit of slavery leading to fear again, but you have received a spirit of adoption as sons by which we cry out, 'Abba! Father!'"

Day 10: The Promise of Following Jesus

Mark 1:17 (NAS95)

"And Jesus said to them, 'Follow Me, and I will make you become fishers of men.'"

Day 11: The Promise of a Seal

Ephesians 1:13-14 (NAS95)

"In Him, you also, after listening to the message of truth, the gospel of your salvation – having also believed, you were sealed in Him with the Holy Spirit of promise, who is given as a pledge of our inheritance, with a view to the redemption of God's own possession, to the praise of His glory."

Day 12: The Promise of Unity

John 17:11 (NAS95)

"I am no longer in the world; and yet they themselves are in the world, and I come to You. Holy Father, keep them in Your name, the name which You have given Me, that they may be one even as We are."

Day 13: The Promise of Peace with God

John 14:27 (NAS95)

"Peace I leave with you; My peace I give to you; not as the world gives do I give to you. Do not let your heart be troubled, nor let it be fearful."

Day 14: The Promise of a Teacher

Luke 12:11-12 (NAS95)

"When they bring you before the synagogues and the rulers and the authorities, do not worry about how or what you are to speak in your defense, or what you are to say; for the Holy Spirit will teach you in that very hour what you ought to say."

Day 15: The Promise of Calling

Ephesians 4:1 (NAS95)

"Therefore I, the prisoner of the Lord, implore you to walk in a manner worthy of the calling with which you have been called."

Day 16: The Promise of Forgiveness

1 John 1:9 (NAS95)

"If we confess our sins, He is faithful and righteous to forgive us our sins and to cleanse us from all unrighteousness."

Day 17: The Promise of the Peace of God

Philippians 4:6-7 (NAS95)

"Be anxious for nothing, but in everything by prayer and supplication with thanksgiving let your requests be made known to God. And the peace of God, which surpasses all comprehension, will guard your hearts and your minds in Christ Jesus."

Day 18: The Promise of Rest

Matthew 11:28-30 (NAS95)

"Come to Me, all who are weary and heavy-laden, and I will give you rest. Take My yoke upon you and learn from Me, for I am gentle and humble in heart, and you will find rest for your souls. For My yoke is easy and My burden is light."

Dr. Jerry D. Ingalls

Day 19: The Promise of an Anointing

1 John 2:20 (NAS95)

"But you have an anointing from the Holy One, and you all know."

Day 20: The Promise of the Ministry of Reconciliation

2 Corinthians 5:18-19 (NAS95)

"Now all these things are from God, who reconciled us to Himself through Christ and gave us the ministry of reconciliation, namely, that God was in Christ reconciling the world to Himself, not counting their trespasses against them, and He has committed to us the word of reconciliation."

Day 21: The Promise of the God of Peace

Philippians 4:8-9 (NAS95)

"Finally, brethren, whatever is true, whatever is honorable, whatever is right, whatever is pure, whatever is lovely, whatever is of good repute, if there is any excellence and if anything worthy of praise, dwell on these things. The things you have learned and received and heard and seen in me, practice these things, and the God of peace will be with you."

Day 22: The Promise of Intercession

Romans 8:34 (NAS95)

"Christ Jesus is He who died, yes, rather who was raised, who is at the right hand of God, who also intercedes for us."

Dr. Jerry D. Ingalls

Day 23: The Promise of Transformation

Romans 12:2 (NAS95)

"Do not be conformed to this world, but be transformed by the renewing of your mind, so that you may prove what the will of God is, that which is good and acceptable and perfect."

Day 24: The Promise of Good Works

Ephesians 2:10 (NAS95)

"For we are His workmanship, created in Christ Jesus for good works, which God prepared beforehand so that we would walk in them."

Day 25: The Promise of the Father's Discipline

Hebrews 12:10-11 (NAS95)

"For they disciplined us for a short time as seemed best to them, but He disciplines us for our good, so that we may share His holiness. All discipline for the moment seems not to be joyful, but sorrowful; yet to those who have been trained by it, afterwards it yields the peaceful fruit of righteousness."

Day 26: The Promise of Freedom

Galatians 5:1 (NAS95)

"It was for freedom that Christ set us free; therefore keep standing firm and do not be subject again to a yoke of slavery."

Day 27: The Promise of Power

Acts 1:8 (NAS95)

"But you will receive power when the Holy Spirit has come upon you; and you shall be My witnesses both in Jerusalem, and in all Judea and Samaria, and even to the remotest part of the earth."

Day 28: The Promise of Greater Works

John 14:12 (NAS95)

"Truly, truly, I say to you, he who believes in Me, the works that I do, he will do also; and greater works than these he will do; because I go to the Father."

Day 29: The Promise of Completion

Philippians 1:6 (NAS95)

"For I am confident of this very thing, that He who began a good work in you will perfect it until the day of Christ Jesus."

Day 30: The Promise of Fruitfulness

John 15:5 (NAS95)

"I am the vine, you are the branches; he who abides in Me and I in him, he bears much fruit, for apart from Me you can do nothing."

Day 31: The Promise of Tribulations

Romans 5:3-5 (NAS95)

"And not only this, but we also exult in our tribulations, knowing that tribulation brings about perseverance; and perseverance, proven character; and proven character, hope; and hope does not disappoint, because the love of God has been poured out within our hearts through the Holy Spirit who was given to us."

Day 32: The Promise of Representing

Ephesians 5:20 (NAS95)

"Therefore, we are ambassadors for Christ, as though God were making an appeal through us; we beg you on behalf of Christ, be reconciled to God."

Day 33: The Promise of Stillness

Psalm 46:10 (NAS95)

"Cease striving and know that I am God; I will be exalted among the nations, I will be exalted in the earth."

Day 34: The Promise of Waiting

Isaiah 40:31 (NAS95)

"Yet those who wait for the LORD will gain new strength; they will mount up with wings like eagles, they will run and not get tired, they will walk and not become weary."

Dr. Jerry D. Ingalls

Day 35: The Promise of Comfort

2 Corinthians 1:3-4 (NAS95)

"Blessed be the God and Father of our Lord Jesus Christ, the Father of mercies and God of all comfort, who comforts us in all our affliction so that we will be able to comfort those who are in any affliction with the comfort with which we ourselves are comforted by God."

Day 36: The Promise of Serving

John 13:15-17 (NAS95)

"For I gave you an example that you also should do as I did to you. Truly, truly, I say to you, a slave is not greater than his master, nor is one who is sent greater than the one who sent him. If you know these things, you are blessed if you do them."

Day 37: The Promise of Abundance

2 Corinthians 9:8 (NAS95)

"God is able to make all grace abound to you, so that always having all sufficiency in everything, you may have an abundance for every good deed."

Day 38: The Promise of Conforming to His Image

Romans 8:29-30 (NAS95)

"For those whom He foreknew, He also predestined to become conformed to the image of His Son, so that He would be the firstborn among many brethren; and these whom He predestined, He also called; and these whom He called, He also justified; and these whom He justified, He also glorified."

Dr. Jerry D. Ingalls

Day 39: The Promise of Joy

John 15:11 (NAS95)

"These things I have spoken to you so that My joy may be in you, and that your joy may be made full."

Day 40: The Promise of Love

1 John 3:1-2 (NAS95)

"See how great a love the Father has bestowed on us, that we would be called children of God; and such we are. For this reason the world does not know us, because it did not know Him. Beloved, now we are children of God, and it has not appeared as yet what we will be. We know that when He appears, we will be like Him, because we will see Him just as He is."

Dr. Jerry D. Ingalls

ABOUT THE AUTHOR

Jerry D. Ingalls serves as the Lead Pastor of First Baptist Church of New Castle, Indiana. He is an ordained minister and has been serving ABC-USA churches in pastoral ministry since 2003. Prior to serving in pastoral ministry, Jerry honorably served in the US Army as an Infantry Officer with assignments in the 82nd Airborne Division and the US Army's World Class Athlete Program, earning awards such as the US Army Ranger Tab, Airborne Wings, Air Assault Wings, and the Expert Infantryman Badge. Additionally, Jerry served as a Chaplain Candidate and graduated from the US Army Chaplain School (2007). He has earned a Doctor of Ministry (DMin) in Pastoral Studies from Grace Theological Seminary (2020), a Master of Divinity (MDiv) from Fuller Theological Seminary (2008), an MS in Counseling and Student Development from the C.W. Post Campus of Long Island University (2000), and a BS in Psychological Engineering from the United States Military Academy at West Point (1996). Jerry was a 1996 Academic All-American athlete at West Point and still holds the Academy and Patriot League records in the hammer throw. He married Kimberly in 1999 and by God's grace they have been blessed with three wonderful children – Beorn, Alana, and Willow. Jerry enjoys reading with his children, camping with his family, backcountry hiking, trail running, and competing at the master's level in track and field. He is also the author of the *Seize the Moment* devotional series.

Dr. Jerry D. Ingalls

Dr. Jerry D. Ingalls

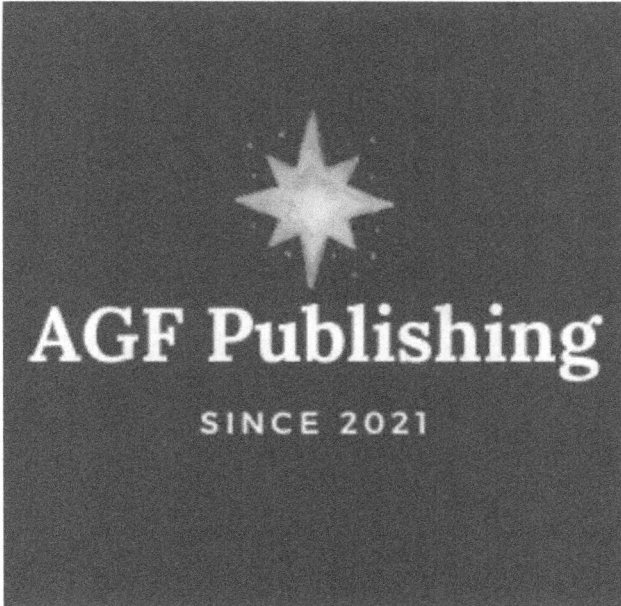

AGF PUBLISHING, LLC

We publish books and media in an array of genres, always aiming to entertain, educate, inform, and inspire people of all ages and reading levels. We encourage and train writers from all backgrounds to work with us in bringing their stories and knowledge to a worldwide audience.

Learn more about the company and all of its offerings at www.agfpublishingcompany.com

Dr. Jerry D. Ingalls

AN AGF PUBLISHING IMPRINT

NORTHSIDE BOOKS & MEDIA
AN AGF PUBLISHING IMPRINT

Northside Books & Media encourages and equips Christians worldwide through fiction and nonfiction. Look for more titles, author information and call for manuscripts at

https://agfpublishingcompany.com/northside-books-media/

Dr. Jerry D. Ingalls

Live Like a Champion Today!